CW00376519

THE COMPLETE CHUB ANGLER

ALSO BY KENNETH SEAMAN

Canal Fishing
Big Fish From Small Waters

THE COMPLETE CHUB ANGLER

by

Kenneth Seaman

DAVID & CHARLES

NEWTON ABBOT   LONDON   NORTH POMFRET (VT)   VANCOUVER

ISBN 0 7153 7310 2
Library of Congress Catalog Card Number: 76-48822

Set in 11 on 13 pt Baskerville
and printed in Great Britain
by Latimer Trend & Company Ltd Plymouth
for David & Charles (Publishers) Limited
Brunel House   Newton Abbot   Devon

Published in the United States of America
by David & Charles Inc
North Pomfret   Vermont 05053   USA

Published in Canada
by Douglas David & Charles Limited
1875 Welch Street   North Vancouver   BC

Introduction

This book is not merely a treatise on the practical arts of angling. It also expounds a philosophy of success based on a sound understanding of the species in relation to its environment, the practice of the essential skills of watercraft and an imaginative use of baits and methods. It also shows how it is possible not only to achieve a high degree of selectivity but also a standard of consistency not normally reached by those who fish in a haphazard way. Well-known but none the less important methods of float fishing and legering could not be left out but are examined in relation to their special application to the needs of chub fishing. In addition, chapters have been included on the little-used but fascinating arts of chub hunting, surface fishing, fly, lure, and nymph fishing in rivers, streams and still waters, together with chapters on the natural history of the chub and specimen hunting, which will be of interest to all who wish fully to understand this most fascinating fish.

K.S.

Natural History

DISTRIBUTION AND HABITAT

The chub is native to most rivers throughout Europe and the British Isles but is not found in Denmark, Sicily, Ireland, the north of Scotland, parts of west Wales and Cornwall. Some of Britain's most famous rivers, such as the Hampshire Avon, Dorsetshire Stour, the Great Ouse, the Wye, the Severn, the Kennet, the Thames and the Swale, all contain large numbers of chub, some of which reach specimen size.

It was once thought that the species was essentially a river fish but it is now known that it can adapt itself to both still waters and canals. It inhabits many different types of swim but specially favours overgrown swims which contain hiding-places into which it can retreat when alarmed.

A favourable environment is all-important to the chub and if there is any alteration in that environment—as when floods or dredging result in the removal of weeds or debris—it will often move on to another more favourable swim.

NOMENCLATURE

The chub (*Squalus cephalus*) is a member of the carp family *Cyprinidae* and it is thought that its name was partly due to the large size of its head and generally 'chubby' appearance. In the northern counties of England it is still sometimes referred to by its colloquial name 'skelly' and in many old angling books the names cheven, chevin, chavender, and cheuene are frequently used. German names for the species include scholl, alet, myn, mouen and schapfisch.

In the United States some forty different species are commonly called chubs. Included in this list are thirty-four species of minnows (*Cyprinidae*), two species of suckers (*Catastomidae*), and three species of cisco (*Salmonidae caregonus*). Several American chubs are similar in appearance and habit to the European chub, notably the fallfish (*Sematilus corporalis*). Although it does not attain the size of the true chub, it will take many of the baits used to catch *Squalus cephalus* and builds a nest which is sometimes 5ft in diameter and 2–3ft high.

CHARACTERISTICS

Description

A powerful-looking fish, with a characteristic blunt head and thick back, the chub is capable of bursts of surprising strength and speed. When young, it is sometimes confused with the dace (*Leuciscus leuciscus*), though several distinctive features should ensure correct identification. The dorsal and anal fins of the chub have a *convex* edge, whereas the dace's dorsal and anal fins have a *concave* edge. The head of the dace is thinner and sharper, too—more like that of a roach—and its flanks are usually more silvery than the chub's.

The colouring of the chub varies slightly, different rivers producing variations in the colour of its back and flanks. The back is usually olive-green or greenish brown, the flanks dull gold or bronze, but in some rivers its back is a lighter shade of green and its flanks dull silver. The pectoral, caudal, and dorsal fins are usually a dull neutral colour and the anal fins pink or coral. The anal fin has three hard and nine or ten soft rays; the dorsal fin has three hard rays and eight or nine soft rays. The pectoral fin one hard and sixteen or seventeen soft rays.

The scale count can also be used to identify the species. The chub has 44–6 scales along its lateral line, with eight or nine rows above it and four or five rows below it. Its distinctive thick, white lips, typical of the chub, can sometimes be seen when the fish itself is invisible.

Size And Weight

Linneas (1758), claimed that the chub of Eastern Europe reached an average weight of 8lb, with individual specimens weighing as much as 16lb. If these weights are accurate, they are exceptional and certainly do not represent the normal average weight attained by chub elsewhere.

In most British rivers the average adult chub measures between 16–18in and weighs between 2–3lb. In the best rivers the average size is larger and individual specimens attain weights of 5–6lb. Really outstanding fish between 6–8lb are comparitively rare and would certainly be more than 2ft long. Not every river is capable of producing specimens of this size since the factors that contribute to high growth rates are by no means common to all waters.

Growth Rates

During their early years chub usually grow slowly. Linneas quotes a length of 2–3in during the first year, 4–5in during the second and 6–9in during the third. More recently, Dr J. B. Leeming of Liverpool University, who chose as a subject for study the chub of the river Welland in Lincolnshire—a slow-moving river, rich in algae and filamentous weed—also found that the growth rates were slow during the chub's early years. Two chub, nearly a year old, were only 1in in length. This comparatively slow growth rate accelerated from the second year on until the chub reached a length of approximately 10in and were about six years old. At this stage growth rates slowed down again but the chub continued to increase in weight, so that while the older fish were roughly the same length as the younger fish they were much fatter and heavier.

Growth rates were most rapid between May and October.

The male chub matured at 3–4 years and lived to be about twelve. Females matured later, at five or even six years, and lived longer than the males. The majority of chub over ten years of age were females. Spawning took place in July rather than during the normal period of April–June and Dr Leeming thinks that this late spawning might partly explain why the chub were so small at the end of their first year. Other species attained lengths of 3–4cm before the chub had hatched out.

Five hundred chub of all sizes were examined, the largest of which was seventeen years old and weighed 5lb, probably the upper limit of growth in this stretch of the Welland in Dr Leeming's opinion.

Research carried out in Germany revealed a marked variation in the growth of chub in different waters. Chub in the small Hermsdorfer river attained a length of 9·5cm in their first year, 11cm in their second year, 17cm in their third year and 23cm in their fourth year. No figures are available for the early years of growth in Hokewarthe Talsperre, an artificial lake, but those for later years indicate a steady increase in weight and length. At the age of six the chub were 24·7cm long, at seven 25cm, at eight 25·5cm, at nine 26cm, at ten 26·2cm, at fifteen 39cm and at sixteen 43cm.

The growth rates of the Hermsdorfer river chub were better than those of the still-water chub. Chub in this little river were larger in their fourth year than those in the lake were in their fifth and sixth years—probably because the river provided more favourable conditions for rapid growth.

The environmental factors most conducive to good growth rates are complex. The depth, clarity, mineral content and average temperature of the water; the amount of weed-growth and animal life it supports; the presence of other food fish and predators, all make important contributions to the total ecology of the water and in many ways enhance or limit the growth rates of the chub.

The Natural Food of Chub

Investigation of the stomach contents of 400 Welland chub revealed that vegetable matter formed the bulk of their diet— especially those fish weighing 2lb or more. The smaller chub, 5–8in long, ate the largest range of organisms.

Caddis, beetle-larvae, mayfly nymphs, stonefly nymphs, shrimps, water-bugs, gastropod molluscs, together with algae and other plant life were eaten by the smaller chub whereas the diet of the larger ones consisted almost entirely of weeds or other fish. In the winter their stomachs were packed with algae but in the summer the leaves and stems of the weeds *Potamogaton* and *Mycrophyllia* predominated. The proportion of stomachs containing other fish was very small, despite the fact that this stretch of the river contained dense populations of food fish. Of those stomachs examined, only twenty-three contained fish remains and of these twelve contained eels. One chub, 16in long, had swallowed a 9in eel tail first! Gudgeon, dace and roach were also consumed in that order of preference.

Dr Leeming's research into the growth and feeding habits of Welland chub has provided much interesting data but a similar investigation carried out in a fast-flowing river such as the Hampshire Avon would almost certainly reveal both different growth rates and different feeding habits. Obviously, there is still room for further research into this interesting subject.

Dr Leeming concludes from his investigations that although chub might eat young salmonids, and also compete to some extent with trout for similar food organisms, they do not compete to the extent that is generally surmised and he does not think that they should be removed from a water unless it is really necessary. It is also the writer's opinion that chub and trout can and do live quite happily together in the same river and will quite often attain specimen size.

Movements and Habits

During the early summer months chub often shoal in large numbers in fast shallow water. It is commonly believed that they do this to clean themselves, but my own observations indicate that they are also attracted by shoals of minnows and, if left undisturbed, they will sometimes remain in the same swim all day, moving upstream and then dropping back again in the manner characteristic of the species.

When the water is extremely low and clear and the sun high, chub often retire to the deepest part of the swim or into some nearby hiding-place, emerging only to feed as dusk approaches.

Changes in the height and colour of the water also influence their movements. When the water is in spate the chub, preferring swims that are slow-moving and shallow, tend to move away from the full force of the faster currents into the side-eddies. If the river overflows its banks they can even be found in the surrounding fields. A fall in the height of the water brings a gradual movement back into the faster water.

Chub are not great wanderers and will often stay in the same swim for a long time. In their infancy they are gregarious and move about in large shoals composed of fish of similar size and age, but as they mature the shoals contain an increasing number of chub of different sizes. This may be due to some extent to uneven growth rates, but also to the infiltration of chub of different age groups. Big chub are not solitary as is often supposed but frequently live in company with many other and smaller fish of their own species. One chub, which I once transferred from its 'home swim' in a stream to a nearby river, returned to that swim and was caught again later in the season, having travelled something like two miles to return to its original home.

When feeding, chub patrol certain familiar routes in the swim and, when sated, retire to their hiding-places, often remaining there for long periods. The number of feeding-sessions is variable and closely related to the temperature of the water and the availability of the different food organisms. Chub can abstain from eating for long periods—which partly explains why they are often so difficult to tempt—and unlike barbel, gudgeon and loach are not typical bottom feeders, though much of their food is taken off the bottom.

SENSES

Vision

The visual acuity of chub is certainly comparable with that of other Cyprinid fishes, which can perceive a wide range of colours, brightness, form and size. They can also discern objects on the bank, though this ability decreases when the water is coloured or when the surface mirror is broken by wind. Its eyes which, unlike the pike's, are positioned on each side of its head enable it to see objects on either side of it as well as in front and it undoubtedly locates much of its food by sight.

Smell and Taste

The chub's olfactory sense is highly developed as in all Cyprinid fish and experiments have shown that they can detect odours at extremely low levels of concentration in water and are thus able to locate food before it is actually visible to them. The odours are detected by two nostrils located one on each side of the frontal part of the head, above and behind the upper lip. These nostrils also enable the chub to discriminate between the waters of different rivers and streams, to detect alarm substances produced by damaged fish, to select different waterplants for food and to identify the sex of other chub.

The sense of taste—which is different and only comes into operation when food is taken into its mouth—is very sensitive, the threshold for sweet substances being much lower than that of man. Whether chub are capable of detecting the odour of tobacco transferred to baits by handling has long been a subject of debate. There is evidence to suggest that they most probably can and it may well be that this taint of tobacco, or other human odours, may be partly responsible for some failures to catch them.

Hearing

Sound is conveyed more rapidly through water than through the air and water at 20°C will carry sound four times faster than air at a comparable temperature. Thus noise made on the bank and transmitted by vibration to the water will probably scare away every chub, as well as most other species, in the immediate vicinity—especially in the smaller rivers and streams—whereas other sounds, such as shouting or whistling, are undetectable since they are dispersed through the air.

Sound in the water is detected through the medium of the chub's lateral line which is extremely sensitive to minute amounts of water displacement and to underwater vibrations. A weight dropped into the swim, or even a smaller fish swimming nearby, will be detected immediately. Experiments have proved that even blind Cyprinids are able accurately to locate objects in the water, though this ability is lost if the lateral line is removed.

Conditioned Responses

To refer to intelligence in relation to fish is a risky procedure but experiments with Cyprinids have proved beyond question that they can be taught to distinguish between circles, squares and triangles. This ability to distinguish between one shape and another is attributed to a 'conditioned response' built up after a variable number of presentations which is rarely less than ten or more than eighty, and usually about thirty. Their ability to learn is accelerated if some form of shock accompanies the experiments; but although individual fish learn more quickly and remember longer, it would seem that the species as a whole is incapable of any permanent retention of experience.

That chub can and do learn from experience is well-evidenced by this account sent to me by angler-author, Peter Wheat, who has an intimate knowledge of river Avon chub:

> Royalty chub are something of an enigma. During the summer the river here is low, extremely clear, and the chub can be seen swimming about in small shoals under the bank. Now I am not exaggerating when I say that these chub, which often pass through the barbel slacks during the day, are completely fearless. It is possible to stand on the bank edge, even in a white shirt, and observe them as if in an aquarium. Sometimes these chub are average shoal fish, up to four pounds; other shoals will contain an odd five-pounder, and still others consist mainly of five-pounders. Once in a while fish come by which are truly eye-popping, and I have seen fish of this calibre which would have weighed six, seven, or even eight pounds.
>
> Here though, where they can be seen and success would seem easy, they are very difficult to catch. The usual ploy is to shower the water where the chub are with loose maggots. In come the chub, feeding like mad, in a frenzy of activity even; but present a maggot to them on light gear, float or loose line, and when the rest have all been gobbled up the one on the hook will still be there like a sore thumb. If you keep up the ploy long enough the chub become wary and remain just on the outer edge of the slack where their shadowy forms can be seen cruising up and down. Of course, chub do get taken like this sometimes—I've caught them myself—but every one costs about a gallon of maggots.

Several interesting aspects of chub behaviour are revealed in this account: the intermingling of chub of different sizes; an ability to discriminate between maggots thrown in as feed and the maggot on a hook; and a display of indifference to the presence of anglers on the bank. Observations of this kind are illuminating if only because they reveal how easily the angler can be deceived into thinking that the chub are not feeding when, in fact, they are simply refusing only the bait that is on the hook.

B

PARASITES

In September 1963 Richard Walker discovered that chub in the Hampshire Avon were infested with the parasite *Pomphorlynchus laevis* and examined the effect these had on chub in an article entitled 'Killer Parasites of the Avon', which appeared in the 20 November 1964 issue of the magazine *Fishing*. The subject was also discussed by Dr James Chubb of Liverpool University's department of zoology in a paper presented to the Coarse Fish Conference and reprinted in *Fishing* in May 1967.

The parasite resembles an orange-coloured maggot and infestation results in the chub losing weight and eventually appearing thin and emaciated. The life cycle of the parasite covers three phases. The adult parasites first infest the chub, shelled acanthors are then produced in the females and are passed into the river by the chub. The intermediate host is the freshwater shrimp, *Gammarus pulex*, which eats the acanthors and is then itself eaten by the chub, thus completing the cycle.

Control of the parasites by chemical treatment or by elimination of the intermediate host, the shrimp, does not seem practicable but it is assumed that the infestations eventually decline naturally.

EDIBILITY

The chub is not a gourmet's fish, its flesh having been described as being like cotton-wool. Ausonious, the ancient Greek writer, referred to it as a fish 'completely stuffed with awn-like bones, a fish which will not keep long for the table.' Dame Juliana Berners, however, had a higher opinion of the chub's culinary qualities. 'The chevin,' she wrote, 'is a stately fish, and his head is a dainty morsel.'

In medieval times various strong sauces were often used to make the chub more palatable. One fifteenth-century recipe advised that the 'Cheune should be served with verjuice and cinnamon, or with gelly, whyte and rede.' Directions given to household staff instructed the servant to 'syne [carve] that cheven'—the chub being part of a second course which included 'congre, samon, dorey, brytte, turbot, halybut, trout, elver, lampreys, and tench in gelly.'

One of the most comprehensive recipes for preparing chub for the table is given in Izaak Walton's *The Compleat Angler*. After revealing that ' . . . the French esteem him so little they call him "un villain" . . .' Walton proceeds to tell his companion, Venator, how to prepare the chub, adding 'Though chub be, by you and many others, reckoned the worst of fish, yet you shall see I'll make it a good fish by dressing it.'

> First scale him, and then wash him clean, and then take out his guts; and to that end make the hole as little, and near to his guts as you can. Especially make clean the throat from grass and weeds that are usually in it, for if that not be clean if will make him taste very sour. Having done so, put some sweet herbs into his belly, and then tie him with two or three splints to a spit and roast him, basted often with vinegar, or rather verjuice and butter, with a good store of salt mixed with it. Being thus dressed you will find him a much better dish of meat than you, or most folks, do imagine; for this dries up the fluid watery humour with which chub do abound.

Nowadays the chub is rarely eaten, the availability of trout, salmon and a wide range of more palatable sea-fish having relegated it to a position from which it is not likely to be resurrected.

SOME MISCONCEPTIONS

It has often been said that chub prefer overgrown swims because of the supply of caterpillars and other insects that fall into the water, whereas, in fact, their liking for such places can be more accurately attributed to the shelter which the overhanging vegetation provides. Even in winter, when the leaves have fallen and the caterpillars have turned to chrysalids, chub can still be found beneath overhanging bushes and trees.

Another misconception is the chub's reputed ability to shed a hook by biting on a root or weed-stem. Shed it, it may indeed do, but what usually happens is that the chub darts over or round a snag and then, checked suddenly by this obstacle, twists or turns so that the direction in which the hook is being pulled is reversed. If this happens—as it often does—the hook flirts free and becomes embedded in the snag. I have watched this happen on several occasions and am sure it is the correct explanation for something that has puzzled chub anglers for a long time.

2

Modern Chub Angling

The keen chub angler is often a solitary individual who stalks his quarry with rod and line, but when the need arises he knows how to wait, too. A versatile man, capable of adapting his tactics to the small overgrown stream, the big river, or the still water or canal, he is above all a specialist with a great respect for the chub and a thorough understanding of its nature and habits.

Angler, artist and writer, Bernard Venables, has described the chub as a fish that sometimes inspires in an angler 'a kind of desperate fanatiscism.' Richard Walker says: 'It is one of our best sporting fishes, which, if less discriminating than the trout, is much warier, and less tolerant of a clumsy approach.' Peter Wheat has a high regard for the chub, too: 'No other fish has given me so much pleasure and excitement, or inspired in me so much respect,' he writes.

The scorn that is sometimes heaped upon the chub stems mostly from ignorance of the true nature of the fish. Hooked in a strong current or close to a snag, a chub will test the strongest tackle. Even in summer when it is supposed to be in poor condition, a chub hooked in a weedy or snaggy swim is no mean adversary, as many anglers without sufficient regard for its strength often discover to their cost. As Sheringham once wrote: 'A strike, a rush, and then alack, a shotless, hookless line is fluttering in the wind.'

HOW TO BECOME A SPECIALIST
The basic essentials of successful chub angling are not diffi-

cult to define. They are a sound understanding of the nature
and habits of the fish, an intimate knowledge of the river, an
ability to select the most effective bait and knowing those times
when the various possible combinations of bait and method are
most likely to produce results.

The technical skills are relatively easy to acquire. Within a
comparatively short time even a novice can be taught how to
present a bait reasonably well on float or leger tackle. The bait
is usually a maggot, and the style of fishing such that it is no
more likely to produce chub than any other fish.

This style of fishing is popular because it sometimes produces
large mixed catches of fish and usually more quickly than any
other method and bait. It is not, however, angling in the fullest
sense of the word, since it can be done—and quite often is—
without any real knowledge of the water and the habits of the
fish and with no specific quarry in mind. Many anglers develop
great technical skills, but comparatively few acquire that deep
understanding of fish and water that enables them to catch one
particular species consistently. Such knowledge takes time,
study and much thoughtful angling to acquire but is the
foundation upon which all good angling is built. Without it
consistent success is impossible because the angler who does not
understand chub cannot hope to become very successful at
catching them. He might, with luck, occasionally catch large
quantities of them or even the odd specimen fish, but to the end
of his days he will still believe that he can only catch them when
the water is 'right', conditions are favourable, the chub are 'on'
and he is in luck.

The specialist chub angler has a different approach. Luck
plays little part in his success which is based upon the practice
of certain simple but essential principles which can now be
listed in order of importance.

Location
Understanding of the habits of the species apart, the ability

to locate chub accurately is possibly the most important of all the chub angler's assets. All fish intermingle to a certain extent but in most rivers there are swims in which chub are more numerous. These swims might be deep swirling holes beneath overhanging trees and bushes, hidden undercuts in high clay banks, or other hiding-places beneath tree-roots, mats of debris, or beds of weed. Where the river is featureless chub can be located by observation, exploration and by choosing a selective method and bait.

In the early stages it is helpful to map each stretch of river, marking the place in each swim where chub have been seen or caught and noting carefully the prevailing weather conditions and water height. If this is done methodically over a long period the angler will gradually learn where chub are most likely to be in the different conditions and where they are most likely to feed.

Chub are influenced by many different factors: the height and colour of the water, the amount of light penetration, their need for oxygen and the availability of the foods upon which they feed. During the summer, when the water is often low and clear, they generally prefer the fast-flowing swims but are seldom far away from a convenient hiding-place. Any rise in the height of the water results in their gradual movement away from the fast currents, but as soon as the water begins to fall the chub drift back to their normal positions.

During the winter they generally prefer the deeper water and are seldom seen in fast runs at the head of a swim—although it is sometimes possible to catch them from fast-flowing shallow swims when the river is above normal height and, when the water is low, in the evenings when light penetration is negligible. Each river has its own different characteristics and the keen angler must be prepared to study each one as a separate and different environment.

The formation and contours of the river bed should be studied, too, as they provide important clues to accurate location. Some swims have their deepest part in the centre of the river, others are deeper under one bank, while a few are of even depth throughout. Obviously, any rise in the height of the water will have a different effect on the chub in each of these different types of swim. Chub in those swims that are deepest under one bank will tend to move over towards the shallower side, while those in swims that are deeper in the centre of the river will move in towards the shallower marginal water on *both* sides of the river. Only in swims of uniform depth will these movements be slight (see Fig 1), and unless all these various movements are clearly understood much valuable time will be wasted fishing places that are not likely to hold chub.

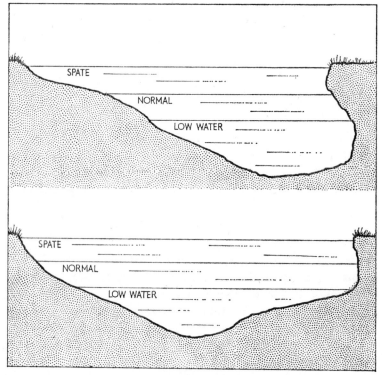

Fig 1   Cross-section of two typical river swims

Light Penetration

Very clear rivers fish best when light penetration is low and the water is coloured. During the middle hours of a summer day, when the sun is high and light penetration at its maximum, few chub will be seen in the shallow slower-moving swims until evening when the light is fading. When the water is low and light penetration at its highest most of the chub will be tucked away in their hiding-places.

At dawn, dusk and on after dark, when light penetration is low, the same shallow swims that were empty during the middle hours of the day will often be alive with chub, and on occasion scores of them may be seen in water scarcely deep enough to cover their backs.

The effects of light penetration are not as marked in those rivers that are normally deep and coloured, but there will still be some movement and the angler should learn all he can about it. In general, the more weeded and deeper swims will hold more chub when the sun is up and the shallower swims more at dusk and when there is a rise in the height of the water.

WATERCRAFT

Watercraft involves the use of a number of natural and acquired skills which, when allied to the other basic requirements of good angling, greatly improve the angler's chances of success.

Stealth and Concealment

The ability to stay quiet and concealed is one of the most important attributes of the successful chub angler—especially when he is fishing the smaller, clearer rivers and streams. Sound, as we have seen, is communicated quickly through water and panics every fish in the immediate area, so that it is essential to move quietly and to make full use of any natural cover that is available. A tree, bush, reed-bed or even a bend in the river is quite sufficient.

Chub are not so easily scared in the larger rivers, but even here the angler who learns to move quietly and approach each swim carefully will often catch more chub than someone who blunders noisily along the banks.

The Observing Eye

An observant angler is always a better angler because he is constantly on the look-out for anything that will enhance his knowledge of the fish and the water. He notes carefully all those places where he sees chub, the position of any snags, weed-beds or undercuts, the places where minnows or other small fish are seen scattering before the assault of a chub, the best method of approach to each swim and the best position from which to cast his bait and land his catch. Gradually the scraps of knowledge gained from his observations are built up until eventually a picture of the river and its fish is formed that is vastly different from the one he had on his first approach to the water. As a result, he fishes with more confidence and a greater likelihood of success than the angler who relies solely upon luck to see him through.

Timing

Chub do not feed all through the day and much of the time the angler spends at the waterside will be wasted unless he can establish through observation and experience those periods when chub are most likely to feed.

Feeding times vary. Chub, like all fish, feed more frequently when the water temperature is raised and less often when it is lowered. The height of the water also affects their feeding habits. In general, they feed least when the water is high and coloured and when it is low and clear. The period following a spate often produces increased feeding activity. When the water is low, feeding activity is usually at its peak at dawn, dusk and on after dark.

If the angler fishes observantly and patiently, learning all he can about the habits of chub, he will gradually learn not only *where* the chub are under different conditions but also *when* they are most likely to feed. The combination of these two important factors can scarcely fail to increase both his enjoyment and the number of chub he catches.

Solitary and Versatile

The keen chub angler is more likely to achieve success if he fishes alone or, at most, with a friend who understands his ways and is of a similar disposition. There will then be fewer distractions and noise on the banks and water disturbance will be minimal. During the course of a season he will fish many different types of swim using many different combinations of method and bait, and the success he achieves will be closely related to his ability to adapt his methods and approach to the particular river he is fishing.

Sometimes he will fish only one swim; on other occasions he will fish many. He may be fly fishing, nymph fishing, dapping, float fishing, legering, surface fishing or hunting, but his bait will always be the one he knows is most likely to be taken by the chub at that particular time and his tackle will be such as to ensure that his bait or lure is properly presented. At all times he will be prepared to improvise, to change both his style of angling and bait to suit the needs of varying conditions of weather and water.

THE CHUB AS A MATCH WINNER

Until comparatively recently chub were not regarded as a match-winning species but this attitude has now changed and winning weights in some rivers have soared, one of the most impressive being a match-winning weight totalling 74lb, all caught with wasp-grub from the river Severn by Ron Baker in 1967. Bags in excess of 20lb are not at all uncommon now and the majority of chub so caught are taken in the course of matches on the larger rivers, such as the Severn, Avon, Trent,

Ouse, Windrush and Swale, where long-trotting tactics com-
bined with heavy groundbaiting do much to overcome the
handicap of crowded banks and the reputed shyness of the chub.

Favourite baits are casters, bread, luncheon-meat and—until
it was banned—the wasp-grub. Some match anglers claim that
once chub have started to feed on the grub they lose all their
customary caution and virtually queue up to take the bait, thus
putting those anglers who do not have the grub at a disadvantage.

Occasionally an angler wins a match without using a scrap of
groundbait, but the general trend—especially for big-river
fishing—is to use it in large quantities. Coventry match-angler
Billy Lane, who has caught 30lb of chub in under two hours,
admits to taking a galvanised bath, 4ft long and filled to the top
with groundbait, for a match fished at Hampton Loade on the
Severn and did not consider this quantity excessive for tackling
this deep fast-flowing water.

The methods used in match fishing vary, long-trotting with a
big quill, cork or balsa-wood float being used for the deep fast-
flowing swims and lighter floats and finer lines for fishing the
slower-moving rivers and canals. Chub hooked on very fine
tackle require careful handling and a flexible rod 13–14ft long
is often used to counter the reduction in line strength.

Legering, in which the swing-tip often plays a prominent
part, is also used and some excellent catches have been recorded
by match-anglers using this method. And although most
matches are usually won by the more experienced anglers, this
is not always the case as evidenced by the achievement of one
angler who, scorning typical match tactics, won a match by
fishing with bread-flake on a No 1 hook and without using any
groundbait! In another match, fished in the river Swale, a ten-
year-old Leeds boy won the match against top-class opposition
by hooking and landing a 6lb 3oz chub on a maggot fished on a
No 18 hook tied to a 2½lb line. The only other fish he caught
was a ruffe!

3

Baits and Groundbaits

Many baits can be used to catch chub but more consistent results can be obtained if the one chosen is that which is most likely to be effective under the prevailing conditions, or when there is some specific reason for preferring it to other baits. It is not good angling to use only one bait in the belief that it is the 'best' bait for chub. Nor is it good angling to change baits frequently. One bait can never be the best for all occasions and the angler who is always changing bait never fishes with any of them long enough to find out whether it is really effective or not.

Each season more chub are caught with lobworms, bread or cheese than any other bait and the angler who uses these consistently throughout the season will certainly catch chub. Nevertheless, it is also true that the angler who uses a greater variety of baits will succeed more often than the angler who uses just a few or only one bait, and there are many baits to choose from, some of which are seldom used by the majority of anglers.

RELATING BAITS TO FEEDING PATTERNS

One way in which the choice of bait can be narrowed down is to relate it to an observed feeding pattern. If the chub can be seen feeding upon some natural food organism it is only simple logic to use that organism or an imitation of it. The fact that so few anglers do this is indicative of how ingrained has become the habit of fishing with maggots or some other equally popular bait.

Minnows and Other Fish

Chub feed on minnows throughout the season but this particular feeding activity can be seen most frequently during the early season when both minnows and chub are active in fast shallow water. In some rivers the colour of the water makes this activity difficult to observe but if minnows are indigenous to that river it is reasonably certain that chub can be caught with them.

Chub will also take other small fish, such as gudgeon, loach, bullheads, small perch and roach, bleak, and even their own fry. Minnows, however, are more numerous in most rivers and for that reason alone are usually preferred to other fish.

Flies

Many flies, including dragonflies, damselflies, craneflies (daddy-long-legs), mayflies, stoneflies, sedgeflies, olives, bluebottles, greenflies and moths are all eaten by chub. They are obviously most deadly as bait when the chub are rising but are always an excellent choice for early season fishing. These natural flies are difficult to catch but ordinary houseflies, which can be bred from maggots, make excellent chub baits. Artificial flies can also be substituted for natural flies and fishing with these will be dealt with in a later chapter.

Nymphs and Shrimps

Many different kinds of nymphs are eaten by chub but they can only be observed feeding on these when the water is very clear. If such activity is observed a nymph, which can usually be obtained by pulling out a quantity of weed, or turning over a stone, should certainly be tried.

Most anglers are familiar with the appearance of the freshwater shrimp which, if it is present in the water at all, is likely to be found in large numbers and is eaten by all fish, including chub. A fine-meshed landing net is useful for catching them.

Weeds

Sometimes chub can be observed gulping in fragments of weed and if they are preoccupied with tiny fragments the chances of catching them are poor. If, however, they are seen to be eating large pieces of silkweed there is always an excellent chance of tempting one of them with this bait.

NATURAL BAITS FOR SURFACE FISHING

In the absence of any discernable feeding activity the choice of bait is not so obvious; but during the summer months when the water is often low and clear some insects that can be found along the river bank or in the fields can prove deadly baits.

The deadliness of grasshoppers was well-known to past masters of the art of chub fishing who often referred to them as 'locusts'. They can be difficult to catch with one's hands but a fine-meshed net will effectively solve this problem and open fields or railway embankments are excellent places in which to find them. Its characteristic buzzing sound, which it makes by rubbing its legs together, aids location.

Beetles can be found under stones, fallen tree trunks and branches, and most kinds of debris. Kept in a tin or jar, they will stay alive for a long time but to avoid unnecessary suffering one should catch only enough for immediate use. Chub love them.

Various species of caterpillars can be found along the river banks. Some prefer trees and bushes for their habitat, others weeds or garden vegetables (unless they have been sprayed). All make excellent baits when chub are in a feeding mood.

Chrysalids, which are the pupae of the bluebottle and common housefly, can be fished on the surface or as a sunken bait. 'Floaters' can be separated from 'sinkers' by placing them in a bucket of water. Many anglers discard the 'floaters' but this is a mistake as chub will often rise to them if they are used in sufficient quantity. They are even more attractive if the bottom part of the chrysalid is carefully peeled away to expose the legs and thorax of the emerging insect.

Another good bait, bread crust, needs no preparation and is most effective when the chub are rising or lying just beneath the surface. Large pieces should be used to lessen the chances of smaller fish taking the bait.

SELECTIVE BAITS

Chub will rise to surface-fished baits throughout the season, but there are many occasions when they are not inclined to rise and when this happens a sunken bait is to be preferred. Many baits can be used for this style of angling, some of the best being those which are more likely to lure chub than other fish.

The angler who uses these baits will not always catch a lot of chub but he will certainly catch very few other fish. For this reason selective baits are excellent for use in rivers which contain many species of fish. They are most effective when the chub can be seen and the bait tossed to them, though this is by no means essential.

Newts and frogs can usually be found wherever there is a shallow weedy pond. They hide under weeds, stones, and debris and when used as bait should be hooked through the skin—not in any vital part of the body—and preferably lowered into the water. If casting, this must be done with care or the bait will easily fly off the hook.

A crayfish is one of the most selective of chub baits but they are not found in all rivers, preferring very clean swift-flowing waters, with plenty of hiding-places. Some fine chub have been caught with this bait.

The black slug is another excellent chub bait which can be found in dewy grass, around old timber and stones, especially after a heavy dew or rain. The finest of all chub baits in the opinion of some anglers is the wasp grub, but they are comparatively little used because of the difficulty of finding nests and extracting the grubs from them. The grubs are sometimes used singly but more often with several on a large hook. Some anglers prefer the 'cake' (that part of the nest which holds the grubs) as it stays on the hook better and can be fished on a large hook and a strong line.

MEAT BAITS

Meat baits, which include sausage, luncheon meat and bacon, can also be used effectively at times but the chub will usually need to be 'educated' to take such unfamiliar morsels by prebaiting. Barbel, too, like meat baits but a measure of selectivity can be achieved by fishing the bait in a well-known chub swim. A large hook should be used and some bigger than average chub have been caught with meat baits.

SEED BAITS

Under this general heading there are a number of excellent but neglected baits which are often effective when chub have grown wary of other more common baits. Quick results should not be expected with these baits; failure is more often due to impatience than to the chub not liking them.

Anglers of long ago used honey to sweeten wheat and saffron to colour it but it is doubtful if this treatment increased the bait's attractiveness. The size of the grain and the correct amount of cooking are more important. A big soft grain will tempt more chub than one that is insufficiently cooked, so that it is advisable to soak the wheat overnight and then cook it very slowly.

Malt, or roasted barley, does not need such a long cooking period and, ideally, should be simmered until it begins to show a firm white centre. Like wheat, it doubles its size during cooking and this should be kept in mind when preparing the bait as

c

it soon sours when the weather is hot. If persisted with, this bait will lure plenty of chub.

Once chub have tasted hemp seed they will often feed on it as avidly as roach. It can be prepared much more quickly than the other seed-baits, twenty minutes' to half an hour's boiling being usually sufficient. If it is cooked too long it will break up and become useless as a hook bait. Once the white shoot begins to show the seeds should be removed from the heat. Chub up to and even over 6lb have been taken with this bait.

Peas, beans and seeds are a somewhat unusual bait for chub, but they can be coaxed into feeding on them. Richard Walker, using butter beans, has caught chub from the Hampshire Avon, some of which, he says, 'were good big ones, with plenty of four pounders, and an occasional five pounder as a bonus.' The tinned products can be used and make easily portable sources of bait.

Though not perhaps as killing as the other seed baits, maize does have one advantage over the smaller ones in that it can be used on a larger hook. A very hard seed, it can only be sufficiently softened by cooking in a pressure cooker for 40min at 13psi and so canned sweet corn is a less troublesome and no less effective alternative. Rice, too, is yet another good seed bait for chub.

A BAIT FOR COLOURED WATERS

The lobworm will catch chub in any river throughout the season. It is, however, the bait supreme when the river is in spate and when it is falling but still coloured.

Lobworms can be collected at night when they come up to lie on the dew-laden grass or, best of all, after a heavy fall of rain. They can also be found in well-manured gardens and sometimes beneath tussocks of grass close to the river. A damp habitat seems essential to them.

OTHER BAITS

Cheese is undoubtedly one of the finest of chub baits and was the favourite of Bill Warren whose exploits with chub on the Hampshire Avon are well known. I tend to use it mostly during the summer and autumn and when the water is at or below normal level, but Peter Stone, who fishes the Thames, has found cheese to be a good bait for chub when the water is coloured, the strongly flavoured Gorgonzola being a favourite choice.

Cheese paste, which is just as effective, can be made by blending cheese with stale bread or dough. There is no reliable evidence to indicate that the colour of the cheese is significant; chub are more attracted by odour than colour.

Bread baits can be used throughout the season but are exceptionally good during the winter when the minnow hordes have ceased to feed. Crust is a fine bait when the water is falling and clearing, while flake is to be preferred when the water is clear. Both should be used in large pieces as chub have large mouths and can gulp in a piece of bread the size of a small orange. If small pieces are used more roach, dace and other smaller fish will be caught. I seldom fish with a piece of bread smaller than a ten-pence piece.

Paste or dough are useful alternatives which have a special application to fast-water legering as they will both stay on the hook longer than flake or crust. Paste of the correct consistency feels smooth and soft and can be jerked off the hook when the strike is made. Hard paste will often be refused or can result in bites being missed.

Maggots have been placed last because they are not selective enough to rate highly as a chub bait. They can, however, be used with reasonable chances of success during the winter so long as the angler does not mind catching other species of fish as well.

A notable exception is provided by the Hampshire Avon where consistent use of the maggot has resulted in the chub preferring them to any other bait. Large numbers of anglers fish this river every year and probably something like 95 per cent of them use maggots. Small wonder then, with this amount of maggots being thrown in, that chub in this stretch of the Avon have become addicted to maggots. Elsewhere in the river the situation is very different and on the Royalty maggots are now banned as bait.

GROUNDBAITING AND PREBAITING

Once the angler has learned to locate chub accurately and to choose the best times to seek them he will realise that it is not always necessary to use groundbait and that he can often catch a chub with his first cast—providing his approach is stealthy. Far too many anglers use groundbait out of force of habit or because of a mistaken belief that it is essential to induce chub to feed. Only when a spell of fishing reveals that the chub are not feeding should groundbait be used.

Groundbait composed of fine particles of bread and meal is not usually the best kind to use for chub as it attracts other, smaller fish. What is wanted is a groundbait that will encourage chub *rather* than other fish to feed and the type preferred by most anglers is usually made up from stale bread, though freshly baked bread is often more effective. When soaked, it emits a milky cloud which diffuses in the current, while the heavier mass of the bread breaks up slowly into large flakes which attract chub from a long way downstream.

For the fast swims a groundbait composed of a mixture of stale bread and a heavy meal, such as wheatmeal, is preferable. Alternatively, paste or dough, ripped up into fragments roughly the same size as the hook-bait, should be thrown into the swim. This kind of groundbait does not attract as many small fish as the fine cloud variety and usually results in a high proportion of chub being caught.

A plentiful supply of groundbait is often necessary when seeking chub in the larger rivers but not for the smaller rivers and streams where the swims are much more confined.

If using other kinds of groundbait it is a good policy to use portions of bait which are roughly the same size as the hook bait. Worms should be thrown in whole, not cut up. Cheese and meat baits should be at least thumbnail size. If it is required to get the groundbait down quickly through a fast current a swim-feeder can be used. Alternatively, a ball of clay or, in the case of cheese and meat baits, a ball of paste or dough containing quantities of the baits will do the job just as well.

Prebaiting, though not essential, is advisable when seed-baits are being used—at least until the chub are feeding on the new bait. If the chosen swim is baited up the previous evening, it is often possible next morning to catch chub from it immediately if the angler approaches it with care. The amount of seeds used should be related to the size of the swim, more being used in the larger swims and less in the smaller ones. Overfeeding can result in the chub refusing the hook-bait.

A study of groundbaiting in relation to chub reveals clearly that they can be encouraged to accept many different baits if they see them often enough and in sufficient quantity. In recent years few anglers have demonstrated this fact so convincingly as the two Derbyshire anglers who took an enormous catch of chub from the river Trent. B. Russell of Ilkeston and F. Woodward of Kirk Hallam caught between them a fantastic catch of chub estimated at between 160 and 170lb. This catch was taken from a swim that had been prebaited with two buckets of wasp grubs, 3lb of cheese and the inside of two loaves. Neither angler caught roach or gudgeon—a significant fact in a river thickly populated with these species. Both anglers used large pieces of cheese or a bunch of wasp grubs as hook-bait.

4

With Fly, Lure and Spinner

FLY FISHING

A certain amount of mystique is still attached to fly fishing but it is by no means difficult to acquire a reasonable standard of casting ability. Success, so far as chub are concerned, is rooted, as it is with bait fishing, in a sound knowledge of the chub's feeding habits, accurate location, a stealthy approach and deceptive presentation of the fly. An ability to recognise the more common flies is helpful but not essential. It is most effective during the summer and in low water conditions will often produce more chub than bait fishing. Dawn and dusk are undoubtedly the best times but chub can be caught on the fly from shady overgrown swims in the brightest conditions.

Choice of rod is very much a matter of individual preference but for ease in casting it is essential to have a matching rod and line. A double-taper line is preferred for lighter, more delicate presentation of the dry fly, but a weight-forward line works the rod better and is more efficient for long casting and for casting into the wind. A tapered leader is to be preferred for dry-fly fishing but a level leader can be used for close-range work in snaggy swims. A shorter, more steeply tapered leader will cast the fly better into the wind.

DRY-FLY FISHING
Choosing the Fly
It would be possible to catch chub by using only one pattern

of fly throughout the season, and indeed, one well-known authority, H. T. Sheringham, has maintained that an angler needed no other artificial fly but the Alder, tied lake size with a kid tail. It is also commonly assumed that chub prefer a large bushy fly but perhaps greater numbers can be caught by using a selection of flies which should include a number of patterns that match as closely as possible those natural insects most commonly seen on the water: a few large dapping flies, a few fancy flies of proven worth and a selection of tiny flies for those occasions when the chub are preoccupied with midges. Such a selection of artificials should include the March Brown, Greenwell's Glory, Iron Blue, Alder, Hawthorn, Wickham's Fancy, Cinnamon Sedge, Damselfly, Mayfly, Flying Ant and Pheasant Tail.

Exact imitation of the natural fly is seldom necessary but if the chub are rising to a hatch of fly it would be foolish not to try an artificial with the closest resemblance. Experience has also shown that flies tied on size 14, 16, or even 18 hooks, will often rise more chub in conditions of low, clear water than the larger flies.

The tiny imitations of midges or flying ants are obviously more effective when the chub are feeding on them but they will sometimes lure chub in bright low-water conditions when nothing else will.

Really big flies, tied on No 6 or 8 hooks, are taken more readily at dusk when light penetration is low and the strong cast which must be used to present these flies is less obvious. After dark it is usually unnecessary to use a finely tapered leader or to restrict oneself to small flies. Any fly with white hackles or wings, such as a White Moth, Butterfly or Coachman, is worth trying at dusk, if only because they are more easily seen.

The dry fly can be tried at any time but is more likely to succeed when chub are actually rising to take flies from the surface and when they are lying above mid-water level. When they are lying close to the bottom the odds are against success in tempting them up.

Upstream Casting

Upstream casting is most effective where lack of cover makes any other approach unwise. The use of a tapered leader and a well-hackled fly will allow the chub more time to discern the fly and so increase the chances of it being accepted. No part of the line or leader should be allowed to fall across the chub or it will almost certainly be put down. Ideally, the first cast should be made diagonally so that the fly alights on the water slightly upstream of the fish.

When the chub cannot be seen it is a wise tactic to cover the rear of the swim first and then gradually to lengthen the casts so that the limit of each is advanced a little at a time. Done carefully and methodically, this will avoid scaring those chub lying to the rear of the swim and is a particularly important procedure to observe when fishing those shallow glides where chub often shoal at dawn and at dusk.

Faster-flowing swims must be fished in a more rapid manner as the current quickly carries the fly back downstream. Always work up the slower-moving currents at the downstream end of the swim first, casting the fly progressively upstream until the head of the swim is reached, meanwhile gathering in line with the left hand to keep in touch with the fly. These fast swims often hold a lot of chub when the sun is full on the water and should not be neglected just because they seem difficult to fish.

Downstream Casting

The downstream cast is obviously most useful for fishing those swims that are difficult or impossible to fish upstream, but can also be used to fish clean, open swims if the approach is carefully made and the angler does not attempt to get too close to the chub.

Presenting the fly without drag can be achieved in several

ways. One way is to pull sufficient length of line from the reel to equal the distance between angler and fish and to drop it in loose coils on the water. Another way is to make several false casts until enough line is out to drop the fly amongst the feeding chub, and then to pull back slightly on the line with the left hand just as the cast straightens out. This causes the leader to fall loosely, allowing a few vital seconds of drift before it straightens out.

The parachute cast is another excellent way of presenting a fly downstream. After making several false casts to get out a sufficient length of line the rod movement is then arrested at twelve o'clock, or in a vertical position, and the casting arm dropped to allow the line to fall loosely on the water. The rod is then gradually lowered forward until it is pointing in the downstream direction taken by the drifting fly.

Casting Across the Stream

This style is not used as often as the upstream style but is often a better method of presenting the fly as chub are less likely to be scared by the line or the leader. One disadvantage is that the current soon creates a 'belly' in the line, but this can be mended by flicking the line back upstream and if the cast is made accurately the chub will often take the fly immediately.

Again, a stealthy approach is essential and false casting should be reduced to a minimum as too many unnecessary movements of the rod and arm will almost certainly scare the fish. A kneeling or crouching position is advisable and when fishing the smaller rivers and streams the angler should stay well back from the edge of the bank.

Dapping

Where overgrown conditions rule out casting, dapping can prove a very effective method of catching chub and one that does not require proper fly-fishing equipment. A bottom-fishing rod, 10–12ft long, preferably made entirely of built-cane or fibreglass, and a fixed-spool reel loaded with 6lb line are all that is required.

The fly is tied to the line and then lowered on to the surface of the water where it should be made to 'dance', either in the erratic circular movements of a fly struggling to achieve flight or in the characteristic up and down movements of an egg-laying fly. If the chub are interested they will soon move up to investigate. When this happens keep calm, allow the chub time to suck the fly in, wait for him to turn down and then hit him hard and hold on. Those first furious struggles may test the tackle to the limit but the chub will soon tire.

Once the swim has been disturbed by the struggles of a hooked fish any other chub in the vicinity will usually bolt for cover, often to reappear later. Meanwhile, another swim should be tried and there are usually many places in the smaller over-grown rivers and streams where this style of fly fishing can be used successfully.

The big bushy flies, such as the Cinnamon Sedge or an imita-tion Damselfly or Dragonfly, are usually best for dapping but I have also had some success with imitation caterpillars, which are tied by winding a strand of black peacock herl in between the longer hackles to imitate the dark centre of the caterpillar. If the chub prefer smaller flies, try a Bluebottle, a March Brown, or a Cochybondhu.

WET-FLY FISHING

Chub will take a wet fly fished in any one of several different ways: lying spent on the surface, hanging just beneath the sur-face film, rising from the bottom to the surface and moving in a jerky, swimming motion imitative of a swimming nymph.

Any number of flies can be used on the leader. My own pre-ference is for a maximum of three for downstream fishing, and usually only one when fishing upstream, but French anglers wielding a rod up to 20ft in length may use up to ten on a very long leader.

The take can be detected if the water is clear enough by watching for signs of a 'boil' or a swirl just beneath the surface and by any unusual check or increase in the speed of movement of line or leader. Tactics of presentation and choice of style will depend on a study of the swim and the observed feeding habits of the chub—if this is possible. Near surface activity will certainly indicate that the flies should be fished shallow while the absence of any visible activity will generally indicate that the deeply fished wet fly is more likely to succeed.

Wet patterns of indigenous flies, such as the March Brown, Iron Blue, Alder and Olives should always be included in the wet-fly selection. Other flies, which do not represent any natural insect but which are extremely useful chub flies, are the Silver or Bloody Butcher, Peter Ross, Alexandra, Zulu, Mallard and Claret. Sometimes chub prefer one of these attractor flies and in the absence of any natural fly they are always worth trying.

Any prevalence of the smaller midges and gnats on the water usually indicates that a very small wet fly, such as a Black Spider, Pheasant Tail or Flying Ant should be tried. It is also worth remembering that a small dry fly, fished just through the surface film, will often lure chub when they are feeding just beneath the surface.

Downstream Casting

Downstream casting with a sunken wet fly must be done properly if it is to be successful. A slack line is first cast up and across the river. The current soon creates a 'belly' in the line and this is corrected by 'mending' the line back upstream. This allows the flies to sink and prevents streaming. Once the flies have reached that part of the swim where the chub are lying the line is checked to bring the flies curving up from the river bed and it is at this stage that they are most likely to be taken.

Another and simple method is to cast the flies upstream close in to the bank and then allow them to travel downstream. As long casting is unnecessary, this is a method a complete beginner can use either with proper fly-fishing equipment or with a flexible bottom-fishing rod and a nylon line.

Upstream Casting

This is an altogether quicker and more active style of wet-fly fishing which can be used in any swim but is most effective in fast broken water. A single wet fly mounted on a 6ft leader is my usual choice, the line must not be allowed to rest on the water too long and a keen eye is needed to detect the take. It is most effective during the early part of the season when the chub are on the shallows or lying between the wavering fronds of weed-beds.

As when dry-fly fishing, greater accuracy in presentation and bite detection is obtained by restricting the length of the cast. Never attempt to cast further than is necessary to reach the chub without scaring them.

Casting Across the River

When the chub are lying across the far side of the river and just under the surface they can sometimes be tempted with a wet fly hanging just beneath the surface film. Any number of flies can be used, but I prefer no more than three which have been thoroughly dampened before casting to ensure quick penetration of the surface film.

The cast is then made upstream of the chub so that the flies drift naturally downstream, the line being 'mended' upstream when necessary to ensure that the flies are not pulled out of position by the current. Takes are usually quite easy to discern, either by actually watching the chub intercept the fly—if the water is clear enough—or by watching the leader for any un-usual movement. The best swims in which to use this method are those smooth-flowing glides which are often found immediately above or below a stretch of fast broken water and which are often deeper under the far bank.

NYMPH FISHING

Nymph fishing for chub is a method comparatively seldom used by coarse anglers, although it has been elevated to a fine art by many trout anglers. Nevertheless it can be a deadly method when the water is low and will often catch chub—even when they are feeding on flies.

Chub will take a wide variety of types and sizes of nymph but most of those I have caught have fallen to either a Pheasant Tail, Iron Blue, Olive, Mayfly or Stonefly nymph, while others have taken unnamed patterns I have tied myself. Exact imitation does not seem important so long as the general nymph shape is adhered to. It is important, though, to carry a selection of weighted and unweighted nymphs, the former for deep fishing and the latter for fishing at or near surface level.

When chub are feeding on midge pupae Geoffrey Bucknall's Footballer is a useful pattern to try and I have also had some success with just a few strands of hen hackle wound round a No 16 hook, and with a very small, partially sunken dry fly. If a dry fly is used it should be sparsely hackled and a Black Gnat, Flying Ant or Grey Duster are excellent patterns to try.

Presenting the Nymph

Successful nymph fishing depends greatly upon matching the presentation and working of the nymph to the feeding pattern displayed by the chub and, in the absence of any apparent activity, to careful and patient fishing of all known haunts.

The methods of presenting the nymph are very similar to those used to present a wet fly. One of the most exciting ways is to cast the nymph to a visible chub and to watch it accept—or refuse it! The cast should be made diagonally upstream with the minimum of false casting so that the nymph pierces the surface gently, just upstream of the chub. An immediate take is always possible but do not be surprised if the chub reacts by darting immediately for cover. This same method should also be used to present an unweighted nymph to chub that are taking the natural ones from the surface.

In the absence of any sign of feeding activity a weighted, deeply-sunken nymph should be used. One method is to cast the nymph upstream and, after allowing it to sink, to work it back downstream in a series of jerky, swimming movements. Another way, most effective in the deep slower-moving swims, is to allow the nymph to sink and then to draw it slowly up to the surface to imitate an ascending nymph, this sink-and-draw movement being repeated as often as is necessary to work the nymph back downstream to a point beneath the rod tip.

A heavily weighted nymph must be used to fish the deep fast-flowing swims, otherwise it will not get down deep enough to be effective. The withdrawal must also be speeded up and is best done by drawing line back through the rod rings with the left hand while at the same time raising the rod. Any nymph

Fig 2   Retrieving a deeply-sunken nymph

taken while it is ascending will be with a real jolt, so a strong leader should be used. (See Fig 2.)

The downstream method of fishing the nymph is similar to that described for fishing the wet fly, the nymph being allowed to sink and progress downstream before the flow of line is checked to bring it curving up to the surface. This method, simple though it is, can be surprisingly effective when the chub are feeding deep and can be done with a bottom-fishing rod and a nylon line.

Whatever method of presenting the nymph is used never hurry over the swim. Fish it patiently and thoroughly, extending the length of the cast each time and watching intently for any unusual movement of the leader. This can happen immediately the nymph alights on the water, when it is being worked back, or while it is being withdrawn. And remember to impart life and movement to the nymph at all times.

LURE FISHING

This is a comparitively new development in chub-fishing technique and there is ample scope for further development. The best known lure is the Polystickle—a semi-transparent imitation of a small fish. Other lures worth trying are Sinfoil's Fry, Perch Fry, Roach Fry, Richard Walker's Barney Google and the Chomper. I have also had some success with an imitation Dytiscus beetle and artificial tadpoles. The tyings of both are as follows:

Beetle. Body of orange silk or floss, ribbed with gold; legs, strands of pheasant wing, or make by carefully cutting them out from each side of the back, which is made of black raffine; eyes (optional), two small, glass beads. A floating version of this beetle can be made from cork or polystyrene.

Tadpole. Body built up with layers of black wool sealed with cellulose varnish; tail, one small blue dun hackle; eyes, two small white beads.

To fish a lure properly it must be activated in a manner imitative of the movements of some natural organism. Some paddle, some dart, some vibrate, some crawl. It is usually most effective when fished slowly and in those places where the chub expect to find the insect or fry that the lure represents.

SPINNING

Spinning is not so selective a method as bait or fly fishing but there are occasions when it is worth trying—particularly when chub are feeding on fry or minnows.

Tackle needs can be met by a spinning rod at least 7ft long and capable of being used with a 4–6lb line, a fixed-spool reel with a high gear ratio for high-speed retrieve in fast water, and a selection of $\frac{1}{2}$–1in spoons and fly spoons. Tactics should be similar to those advised for fly fishing, the nearest water being covered first and the cast gradually lengthened to cover the whole swim.

A fast retrieve is essential when spinning very fast-moving swims but the slower-moving ones can be spun over more slowly. An attractive darting motion can be imparted to the spinner by moving the rod-tip from side to side. The deeper weed-free swims are the easiest in which to spin but fast weeded swims should not be overlooked as they often hold some fine chub and a spinner worked carefully through the clear channels will sometimes tempt one out.

Plate 1. Royalty Fishery, looking upstream towards the Railway Bridge. On the other side of the bridge is the famous Pool from which countless big chub have been taken

Plate 2. The fruits of an evening's dry-fly fishing—seven chub taken on a Greenwell's Glory

Plate 3. The bank on this stretch of river is undercut, so the angler keeps well back and lowers the bait into the water, keeping one hand on the rod ready for a quick strike

Plate 4. Fishing the 'stumps' swim in winter. A chub has taken the bait, the strike has been made, and strong tackle—a Mark IV Avon rod and 8lb line—was essential to bully the chub up out of the roots

5

Hunting and Surface Fishing

The hunting style of angling can be used on any waters but is most effective in smaller rivers and streams in which chub can often be seen, poised darkly in the glass-clear water. It is not a form of angling requiring infinite patience or the use of enormous quantities of groundbait. Rather is the accent on mobility and the careful fishing of every likely spot with one selected bait. Success depends much upon an intimate knowledge of the river and of the times when chub are most likely to be found in open water, the ability to select the most suitable bait for the occasion, and, above all, upon a stealthy and unobserved approach.

Low clear water and brilliant sunshine, conditions which many anglers regard as hopeless, are not always so adverse as is generally supposed since the chub are more easily seen and pinpoint accuracy in presentation of the bait can be more easily achieved. Bearing in mind the need for a well concealed approach, it is best to start fishing at the downstream end of the fishery and to work gradually and carefully upstream, though opportunities to present the bait downstream or even under the rod tip do sometimes occur and should certainly not be neglected.

As a general rule it is better to cover a small amount of water thoroughly than to attempt to cover too much carelessly. Overgrown rivers and streams which twist and turn and offer a constantly changing variety of swims provide the most fascinating fishing but also demand greater concentration and slower progress than the bigger more open rivers. When the hunting style is used the bait is tossed or lowered to the chub and little or no weight is used. It is one of the simplest styles of angling but, properly executed, one of the most effective.

Tackle

Requirements for this style of angling comprise a 10–11ft rod (the Mark IV Avon or carp rods are ideal), a landing-net, a fixed-spool reel loaded with line of at least 5lb breaking strain, a supply of hooks, some weights and the bait. Probably the most important item of this equipment, the rod should be powerful, flexible and capable of handling a large fish. Most rods designed for float fishing are unsuitable but there are many fine legering and specimen-hunting rods that can be used for this style of angling.

Only in exceptional conditions of crystal-clear water and brilliant sunshine should there be any necessity to use any different equipment and then only in snag-free swims. In such an event both rod and line would need to be changed. I use an 8½ft sea-trout rod which is light but resilient, in conjunction with a 3lb line and with this tackle I can handle any average-sized chub caught in open water.

Hooks should be carefully chosen and one of the best is the straight-eyed bronze hook, which has a small eye and a fine sharp point. Silver-or gold-coloured hooks are too conspicuous and can scare chub, especially when the water is very clear.

Minnow Fishing

When chub are actually seen to be feeding on minnows—as they often are in the early weeks of the season—it would obviously be foolish to neglect the opportunities this activity affords.

There are several ways of presenting the minnow. One is to fish it upstream on a weightless line. Another is to drift it downstream on a float tackle. More limited opportunities also occur to lower the minnow down into the swim and actually to watch the chub gulp it in. When they are not feeding in the shallows, or are concealed by the depth of water, the method can still produce results if the angler fishes carefully and patiently up the river, casting or lowering the minnow into every likely haunt.

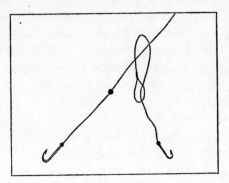

Fig 3   Tackle for use with a minnow bait

The upstream method is most effective and exciting when the chub are feeding on the shallows but it is essential to approach from downstream and to cast the minnow first to the nearest chub. If this is carefully done several chub can be caught from the same swim.

Very fast-flowing swims, such as those situated immediately below a weir or at the upstream end of a shallow stretch of the river, can be fished by drifting the minnow downstream to the waiting chub. An upstream cast is also possible and the angler must decide which position will allow him to make the best use of the available cover.

A little weight is sometimes necessary to sink the minnow, especially in the deeper swims. Weeded swims are best fished by casting the minnow up into the clean runs between the weeds, while overgrown swims are fished by drifting the minnow downstream under the overhanging bushes. A float is useful for this style of presentation but not essential. The main thing is to be prepared to change both the manner and the direction of presenting the minnow as circumstances dictate.

Minnows are easily caught with a maggot or fragment of worm and can be carried in a jar or tin for use as required. Another way which dispenses with the need to carry a jar is to attach a small hook to the reel line by passing the hook round the line and back through its own loop. The baited tackle is then lowered into the swim and once the minnow has taken the maggot it can be transferred from the small hook to the large one—which should be at least No 6 size. (See Fig 3.)

Fishing the Upstream Worm

The upstream worm is another deadly but little used method of catching chub that can be used throughout the season and is especially useful when the water is low and clear. No float is required and it is only necessary to use a weight in fast-flowing swims.

The cast is normally made straight upstream and the worm allowed to fall back naturally with the current while the angler keeps in touch by reeling in slowly. The line between rod tip and bait must never be allowed to become taut or a chub will feel the resistance from the rod tip and promptly eject the bait. It is also a mistake to retrieve line too quickly as this causes the worm to spin. Ideally, a little slack line should be kept between rod tip and bait and a close watch kept for that tell-tale tightening of the line that signals a bite.

Obviously, the best results will be obtained when the water has not been disturbed by other anglers and the most favourable conditions are undoubtedly when the river is fining down after a spate, though the method will catch chub even when the water is down to the stones.

Crayfish and Other Baits

Among the other baits commonly used for this hunting style

of fishing the crayfish is so attractive to chub that it should be tried whenever available. Richard Walker has caught many specimen chub with crayfish and says:

> It is desirable to kill the crayfish first. This you do by giving it a rap with a small priest a little way behind its eyes so as to kill it, and at the same time fracture the carapace. After killing it break off the claws if the crayfish is medium to large size, but leave them if the crayfish is small. The crayfish is put on the hook by sticking the point of the hook through the second segment of the tail, the point going in on the underside and coming out of the upper side. It is very important to see that the whole of the point and an appreciable amount of the bend are standing clear otherwise there will be a lot of misses. For average size crayfish a No 4 eyed, round-bend hook is all right, but use a No 2 for very big crayfish. In my experience it is rare for a chub to take a crayfish after it has reached bottom. I am not suggesting that they never do; only that they prefer to take it either while it is sinking, or when it is being drawn up to the surface.

Some of this advice is also applicable to fishing the black slug, frog or newt, all of which should be used on a large hook. Chub will pick these baits up off the bottom but are more likely to take them if they are cast or lowered into the swim.

If more common baits such as paste, cheese or flake are being used the bite is detected by watching the line, or in very clear water by watching the bait. If it disappears, strike! A chub has probably picked it up and if the strike is delayed the chance will have been missed.

The hunting method also has the attraction of a minimum of bait requirements. With a single maggot or a small worm dug up from a damp place on the riverbank one can catch many minnows and with those minnows go on to catch chub. There are also many other natural baits such as shrimp, caddis, as well as various nymphs and beetles which can be easily caught at the riverside and used. The most successful chub hunters are those who travel lightly and know how to make the best use of the baits readily available to them.

SURFACE FISHING

Surface fishing embraces several different but effective methods which have special application to early season fishing: dapping with live insects, drifting a bait or live insect downstream, or casting a floating bait upstream on a floatless and weightless tackle. Surface-fished baits are especially deadly when the river is low and clear and will often lure chub when baits fished below the surface are ignored.

Dapping with a Live Insect

When the summer sun beats down on the river illuminating every weed-bed and stone and the chub hang darkly in the slow whorls of current beneath the shade of overhanging trees and bushes the live insect, carefully dapped on the surface, will often lure one out. It can be a beetle, a grasshopper, a caterpillar or a live fly. Any of the flies found on or around the waterside can also be used, the crane fly or daddy-long-legs being especially good. Newly-hatched mayflies, dragonflies, or damselflies are also ideal if they can be obtained.

If a beetle is used the hook is inserted under the wing-case and brought through so that the point is exposed. The hook should never be thrust through the beetle's body. A No 6 hook is about right for a large beetle and a No 8 or 10 for a small one. The beetle is presented by lowering it carefully down onto the surface of the chosen swim. No part of the line should touch the water and rod movement should be kept to a minimum. Normally it is not necessary to give additional movement to the beetle as if the chub is interested it will rise slowly to examine the beetle, at which stage it is essential to remain perfectly still or the chub will be off and away. Once it has taken the beetle into its mouth it should be allowed to turn down before the strike is made.

The same tactics apply when presenting a grasshopper or one

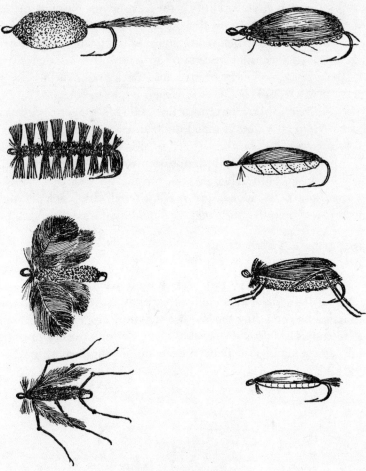

Fig 4   Artificial lures

of the larger flies but a smaller hook should be used to fish a
bluebottle or housefly. This should be carefully inserted just
under the skin of the upper part of the thorax and then brought
through to reveal the point. Caterpillars should always be fished
on a sharp hook and nicked lightly through the skin of the back.

When live insects are unavailable, artificials can sometimes be just as attractive to chub if they are given life and movement by jiggling them on the surface. Some of these artificials can be bought, but below are some of my own tyings which have proved successful. (See also Fig 4.)

Beetle. Body, yellow or orange floss. Back, black raffine. Legs, black fibres from crow or rook wing or split raffine.

Moth. Body, yellow or orange floss. Hackle, ginger or furnace cock. Wings, two small, matching feathers from mallard wing.

Grasshopper. Body, green or yellow silk. Legs, knotted strands from pheasant wing. Back, half-dozen or so similar fibres laid back over the body. Hackle, brown cock.

Damselfly. Body, blue or green silk, ribbed with black peacock herl. Hackle, blue dun. Wings, two matching blue-dun hackles.

Float Fishing with Live Insects

A complete change of tackle is needed to drift a live insect downstream. A 12–13ft rod, a small quill float, a 2–3lb line and a No 12 hook make an ideal combination. Normally the float is attached by threading the line through both rings but resistance is reduced if it is threaded on to the line through the bottom ring only and a small stop tied on each side of the float ring. (See Fig 5.)

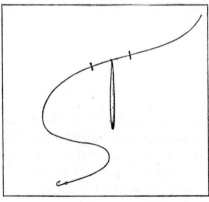

Fig 5 Surface-fishing tackle

When presenting the bait it is advisable to fish from a concealed position and to hold the tackle back slightly until it reaches the feeding area, at which point it should be allowed to drift freely. This tactic will ensure that the line is not taut from float to hook and the fly will drift over the chub naturally and without restraint.

Chrysalids are fished in the same style and although they tend to attract dace, chub will sometimes take them avidly. Such small baits must however be fished on a small hook and a relatively fine line, so that it is best to use a long supple rod and to avoid overgrown, snaggy or weedy swims. Smooth-flowing swims devoid of snags and of only moderate depth are the best for this style of fishing.

It is worth noting here that chub will often accept a live fly or other insect fished beneath the surface when they are disinclined to rise. Float-leger or laying-on methods can be used to sink the fly and in clear water it is often possible to watch the chub take the insect which is often enclosed in an attractive air-bubble.

Surface Fishing with Crust

Both the tackle set-ups recommended for fishing live insects can also be used with bread crust. The stronger tackle and large hook are preferred for long-range fishing and weedy or snaggy swims; the longer rod and float tackle for presenting a smaller piece of crust in clean swims. It is not necessary to use a float with the stronger tackle and if a large piece of crust is used on a hook up to No 1 size the weight of the bait alone is sufficient to pull line from the spool.

If there are no signs of chub rising a few crusts drifted down the swim will often bring them up. It is possible to catch them with this style of fishing at any time of the day and in almost any kind of water conditions but the best time is undoubtedly at dusk when the light is fading and the water suffused with the soft afterglow of sunset. At this magic time chub often work their way up into the shallows and the take is sensed or felt rather than seen. There may have been no intimation that the chub were feeding as the crust is allowed to flow quietly away downstream and out of sight. Then suddenly there is an audible splash, the line tightens and the rod tip goes over in a long shuddering curve. That first lunge of a chub hooked in fast water is extraordinarily powerful, so be prepared.

Fishing the crust upstream calls for a different approach. The same powerful rod, strong line and large hook should be used but as the current cannot be used to carry the bait to the chub it must be cast upstream. As an aid to casting it is advisable to dip the crust in the water first and then to make the cast with a gentle, underhand swinging motion. When the water is low, chub lying in the shallows will sometimes flash up from the bed of the river to take the crust just as they take a fly.

Another advantage of this method is that it is possible to get much closer to the chub and, because the length of the cast is shorter, to attain greater accuracy in casting and striking. Given a take, few chub should be missed.

Dapping the crust is another method which, though little used, will often yield satisfactory results where adequate cover on the banks permits of an unobserved and stealthy approach.

6

Chub in Hiding

LEGERING

There are times when few chub are out in open water and there
are also many swims which, because of their depth, pace and
size can be fished most effectively with a leger tackle. Generally
speaking, legering techniques are mainly used in fast deep
swims where it is necessary to keep the bait steadily in one place,
for fishing snaggy and weeded swims, and when it is too dark for
float fishing.

Tackle

Float-fishing rods can be adapted to legering with a swing-tip
but for all-round efficiency a proper legering rod is to be preferred and is essential for fishing snaggy swims and for long-
range casting with heavy weights.

Legering weights come in many different shapes and sizes
but most needs can be met from a selection of Arlesey bombs,
drilled bullets, coffin and spiral weights, and ordinary split-shot
in AA and swan-shot sizes.

Of the various types of leger rigs employed, the link-leger is
preferred by the majority of experienced anglers, my own choice
being a rig which makes use of two swivels, one as a stop and the
other as a means of attaching the link and its weights to the
reel line. If a strong line is used and the swivels are securely tied
this tackle will withstand terrific pressure. (See Fig 6.)

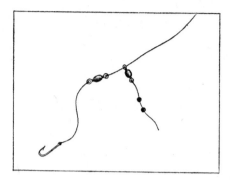

Fig 6   Link-leger tackle using two swivels

Legering Methods

Most swims can be legered by using either upstream or downstream methods and the thoughtful angler makes his choice only after considering which is best from the point of view of concealment, casting and striking efficiency. The under the rod tip style is seldom used nowadays but is still one of the most efficient of all legering methods as the distance between angler and fish is reduced to a minimum and both bite detection and striking are therefore much easier and more effective. It is a particularly useful method for fishing snaggy swims and for fishing close in under a bank.

The length of trail to be used is a controversial subject. Some anglers prefer a trail up to 3ft long—more in some cases—while others prefer only a few inches. One cannot be dogmatic about the matter but if crust is used a short trail is essential; other baits can be fished on a longer trail if desired. The main defect of the long trail is that bite registration is not as immediate as with a short trail. For this reason the shorter trail—about 3–9in—is to be preferred and is essential for legering fast shallow swims. A slow-sinking effect can be achieved with a short trail merely by reducing the weight to the minimum required to sink the bait.

LEGERING THE CLEAN SWIMS

Weed-free swims are comparatively easy to leger; it is only necessary to use sufficient weight just to hold the tackle in that part of the swim where the chub are shoaling. If, for instance, the chub are shoaling in the fastest current, in the centre of the river or perhaps under the opposite bank, sufficient weight must be attached to the leger link to hold the tackle out in this part of the swim. If on the other hand the chub are in the quieter areas of the swim adjacent to the fast current less weight is needed.

This point may not seem of great importance but if the weight is not adjusted to hold the tackle in that part of the swim where the chub are, bites are much less likely to occur and the angler will then mistakenly conclude that the chub are not feeding. As explained in Chapter 2, alterations in the height and colour of the water cause chub to move from one part of a swim to another and this must be kept in mind. Generally speaking, the faster currents should be legered when the water is low and the slacker ones when it is above normal level.

Another small but important point is that the tackle should never be cast directly into that part of the swim where the chub are lying, but rather cast above or beyond them so that it is carried slowly downstream to them by the current. Instantaneous takes are then more likely.

Very slow-moving swims with no appreciable variations in the pace of the current can be legered quite successfully with one weight, which should be just sufficient to overcome the buoyancy of the bait. Baits such as cheese and paste can often be used without any weight at all.

Many anglers fish from a position on top of the bank which allows them a clear view of their tackle, but also allows the chub a clear view of them! It is better to remain out of sight, above any bend in the river and down under the bank if possible. The tackle can then be cast out and across the current and allowed to swing downstream around the bend. It is not necessary to be able to see the tackle; the line or rod tip will give a clear bite indication.

HIDING PLACES AND COUNTER-CURRENTS

In most rivers there are many snaggy places and overgrown swims where chub lurk unseen. Most anglers pass them by but the experienced chub hunter pays them special attention and regards no swim as impossible to fish as long as there is a reasonable chance of getting a bait in and the hooked chub out.

Strong tackle is essential to fish swims of this type successfully. A Mark IV carp rod and a 7–8lb line is not too strong as even a moderate-sized fish can break the line by ensnaring it around an unseen snag. Supple rods and fine lines should never be used to fish snaggy swims.

Wherever drifting masses of weed or debris have accumulated against an obstruction such as a bed of bulrushes, a tree root or a fallen branch, such mats, as they are called, should never be overlooked as they often conceal chub, especially when the water is low and the sun high. Some mats are only temporary hiding-places which the chub will leave once the mat disintegrates. Others may form over a deep hole, weed-bed or undercut into which the chub can retreat when the mat itself disperses. Only long experience of exploring mats will enable the angler to distinguish between permanent chub haunts and those which are only temporary hiding places.

Mats are best fished with the under the rod tip style. The baited leger tackle is lowered quietly into the swim at the upstream edge of the mat and then eased down under it. Sometimes a take comes at once; more often there is a waiting period before the movement of the line signals a bite. When this happens the strike should be made quickly and firmly and the chub 'bullied' away from the mat. Quite often the thrashings of the hooked chub will scare the others and for this reason it is best to adopt a roving style, moving from mat to mat so that each is given a resting period. If this is done it is possible to catch quite a lot of chub, even in the full heat of a brilliant summer afternoon.

Weed-Beds

Beds of weed conceal many chub, too, and no matter how dense they may appear to be there is usually a gap somewhere into which a bait can be lowered or cast. Again, strong tackle is essential to ensure that the hooked chub is successfully landed.

Both upstream or downstream legering can be used in between submerged weeds. The formation of the swim should be studied first, bearing in mind always the need to remain concealed, and it will generally be found best to sit downstream of the weed-bed and to leger upstream. Some false bites may be registered by the movements of the submerged weed against the line but with practice you soon learn to recognise the real thing.

Beds of lilies call for a slightly different technique as both submerged and emergent growths have to be contended with. If there are clean areas of bottom in between the lilies the bait can be legered in between the submerged clumps; but if the bottom is covered with weed the line should be allowed to rest across one of the flat surface leaves so that the bait hangs suspended above the bottom. A clear indication of a bite is given when the line tightens and pulls the leaf out of position—a natural bite indicator that is better than any float.

Sometimes the chub can be seen rising up through the water to take the suspended bait and one can then time the strike exactly. Whatever happens, strike hard and get the fish out quickly or it will almost certainly ensnare the line in the tough lily stems. For this style of fishing it is preferable to sit downstream of the swim and, if possible, to have the sun behind you so that the whole of the swim is illumined.

Undercuts

In many rivers one side is much deeper than the other and the bank on the deeper side is often eroded and fissured with undercuts. When the water is low many chub lie close under this bank and the easiest way to catch them is to use the under the rod tip style and a link-leger tackle. (See Fig 7.)

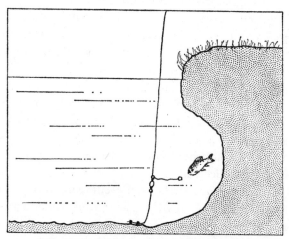

Fig 7   Legering for chub in an undercut

There are several ways of fishing an undercut but experience indicates that it is best to start at the upstream end of the undercut and then work the bait carefully downstream, lifting and lowering the rod tip at intervals to ease the tackle gradually down the whole length of the undercut. At no time should the bait be lifted from the water.

As always stealth in approach and quiet presentation of the bait are essential, so walk quietly and never attempt to look down into the swim first. Push the rod carefully forward out over the edge of the bank and gently lower the tackle into the water, easing line out until the weight touches the bottom. Then put the rod down on the bank with its tip protruding out over

Plate 5. Because the water is very low in this small-river pool, the angler is using an upstream float-leger tackle to hold the bait out under the far bank
Plate 6. Still-water legering in the summer is more likely to bring success if the angler fishes into the wind from a reasonably concealed position. Note how the rod is elevated to allow a slack-line bite to register

Plate 7. A catch of chub taken in one swim by the author on a winter day, using bread-flake

Plate 8. One monster that did not get away. This one topped the 7lb mark, but specimens of this size are exceedingly difficult to catch

the edge. Keep your hand on the rod, or close to it, ready for an immediate strike.

Bites are signalled first by line movement. If this is missed the rod tip will bend over unmistakably but it is best to watch for the line movement as any delay in striking may mean a missed fish. It is also better on most occasions to strike outwards in order to pull the chub away from the undercut. A strike made directly upwards often results in the chub escaping when the tackle gets snagged up in an unseen crevice.

Most undercuts are fished at close range but there are certain swims in which the bait must be legered across the river and under the far bank. This method is rarely as satisfactory as the under the rod tip style because intervening currents tend to pull the bait out of position; but if there is no alternative it is sometimes possible to leger across the river providing the rod is elevated to keep as much line as possible up and out of the current.

Snaggy Swims

The most intimidating places to leger are those that contain fallen branches, roots, masses of sunken debris or dense weedbeds, and which are sometimes overhung by bushes or trees. Chub love these places but exceptionally strong tackle must be used to land them as they are seldom far away from a snag. I generally use a Mark IV carp rod and an 8lb line. Such swims should be carefully studied in advance and the best position from which to fish will usually be the one which allows maximum pressure to be exerted to pull the chub away from the snags.

Typical of the swim which must be tackled in this way is one from which I have caught many fine chub. The upstream end of the swim is spanned by several strands of barbed wire and immediately downstream of the wire a group of hawthorn trees encroach thickly over the swim. The chub can usually be seen lying close to the hawthorns, just downstream of a mass of

E

debris. The rest of the swim is overgrown with streamer weed, leaving a clear channel about 6ft long and 2ft across at its widest point close in to the hawthorns. The only way to fish this swim is to leger upstream from the opposite bank, casting the bait over the weeds.

Tunnels and Weir Pools

Bridge tunnels often conceal chub and are best fished from a downstream position using the upstream legering method. Downstream legering is sometimes possible but in most cases makes it far more difficult to control the chub and there is the additional risk of losing it through the line chafing against sharp edges of the brickwork.

Bites are easy to detect. The first indication is usually given by a sudden tightening of the line. Or the line may fall back downstream at a faster rate than the current, in which case it is necessary to take up the slack line very quickly and make a firm sweeping strike.

Another way of tackling the problem of tunnel fishing is to flick the bait over the parapet but this calls for very strong tackle and the ability to get down on to the bank below very quickly or the chub will almost certainly escape. Everything considered, the upstream legering method is probably the best.

Weir-pools differ considerably in size, bottom formation and strength of current. During the summer many chub lie in the foaming water below the sill and in the faster currents below. A bait legered upstream close to the sill will often tempt some of them, cheese, minnow, and worm being favourite baits for early season fishing.

Quite often a strong current flows back upstream under the surface current and a bait fished on a long trail will be carried back upstream right under the sill where the chub are lying. Bite indication is similar to that given by chub lying under tunnels—a slack line bite that must be hit with a sweeping overhead strike. Downstream legering is possible but will often result in many rapid bite indications that are very difficult to strike successfully.

When the level of the water rises the slacker areas at the edges of the fast currents will repay careful legering with worm or cheese. The deeper, slower-moving parts of the swim usually produce more bites when the river is in spate.

No-one should expect to get consistent results from a weir-pool until the nature of the pool and the habits of its chub have been studied and understood. This takes time and patience and the small pools that are found in many small rivers and streams can be just as fascinating to fish as the larger ones of the big rivers and allow more opportunities for close-range fishing. The lessons learned from studying these smaller weir-pools can then be applied to fishing the larger and more difficult pools of the big rivers.

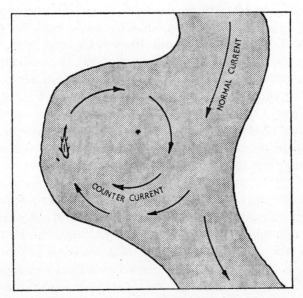

Fig 8 A typical counter-current with chub facing downstream

Counter-Currents

Counter-currents usually occur most frequently at the edges of a fast current and quite often close to a bend in the river. Chub tend to lie in them and with stealthy approach and bait presentation there is always a chance of catching one of them quickly.

The important point to remember is that the undercurrent flows in an opposite direction to the normal current. This means that the chub will be lying with their heads facing downstream and so the swim must be approached accordingly if the angler is to avoid scaring the chub. The larger counter-currents can sometimes be fished in the normal way but the smaller ones that lie close in under the bank should always be approached from an upstream position. (See Fig 8.)

BITE REGISTRATION

Because the chub is a comparatively large fish it is commonly assumed that a bite will always result in the rod tip being pulled over but many fish will be missed if the angler waits for such a positive signal. To pull the rod tip over, the chub must either pick up the bait and swim downstream with it or dislodge the leger weight and this it does not always do. Sometimes it swims upstream with the bait; at other times it will suck the bait in while lying motionless. In each case the only bite registration will be an almost indiscernible tightening of the line and fewer fish will be missed if the strike is made at the first sign of any such suspicious movement.

After dark, bite detection by sight becomes increasingly difficult although it is often possible to see the rod tip for a long time after sunset by cocking the rod up against the afterglow in the sky. Alternatively, a white plastic sleeve can be folded around the rod tip or use made of a luminous indicator or swing-tip. The easiest way to overcome this problem is simply to hold the line, but do not loop it over your fingers or a nasty accident could result when a chub takes the bait.

Peak feeding times for chub often come just after dusk and moonlight not only makes it easier to detect bites but also often stimulates feeding activity, especially when the water is low.

MISSED BITES

Bites are missed on the leger for various reasons. Faults in tackle and bait presentation are responsible for some failures and one should never leger downstream on a tight line or use more weight than is necessary to hold the bait in position.

Slow reaction to bite registration is also sometimes responsible and is a difficult problem to overcome especially when legering fast water when there is an inevitable time lapse between bite detection and striking. Tips to remember are to watch the line at the nearest point to the fish—which is where the line enters the water, to use a bite indicator and to leger upstream rather than down.

Other fish are missed because the chub never takes the bait properly into its mouth but merely dislodges it or the weight and so gives a false bite indication. This happens most frequently in very fast water and small chub are mainly responsible. Again, it is a difficult problem to overcome and the best advice is to strike at every bite indication and not be surprised if you miss most of them.

Legering very fast water can also result in a high proportion of missed bites because the large weight that must be used to hold the bait in position and the pressure of the current against the line combine to create considerable tension and consequently increase the speed of bite registration. One way of lessening the tension is to position oneself, where possible, so that the rod can be pointed straight downstream and to unscrew the tensioner on the reel so that any movement of the leger will cause both audible and visible bite indication. Alternatively, a centre-pin reel can be used if the ratchet is engaged.

7

Float Fishing in Rivers

Float fishing for chub calls for its own particular skills and approach, for while it is basically a static form of angling it is also one in which the angler is constantly casting his float, guiding it down the swim and often striking at long range. Keen eyesight and quick reactions are essential.

It is a method to be preferred to the leger when it is necessary to fish a moving bait over a weeded bottom or when the river is full of drifting weed which would cause false bites to be registered on leger tackle. A properly presented float tackle also allows the angler to work his tackle and bait much further downstream than is possible with a leger and to present his bait in either a slow-sinking or quick-sinking style, close to the surface, at mid-water level or near to the bottom, as required. It is also a particularly effective method for big-river fishing.

No one method of float fishing is suited to all swims or all water conditions. The nature of the swim, the depth and pace of the water, the position of the chub, the depth at which the bait is fished and the manner in which it is presented must all be taken into consideration.

TACKLE

The most suitable type of rod would be one made of fibre-glass or built-cane between 11–13ft long and with sufficient backbone to set a hook at distances of up to 50yd or more when used with a line of 4–7lb breaking-strain. A more supple rod matched with 2–3lb line could also be useful but in most circumstances the stronger tackle is to be preferred—especially for long-trotting in deep strong-flowing water.

The choice of reel is a matter of personal preference. The free-running centre-pin is probably best if the angler wants to fish in the traditional manner with the float restrained so that the bait precedes it but most anglers prefer either the fixed-spool reel or the closed-face reel. Casting is then made much easier and if the spool is correctly filled to within ⅛in of its lip it is possible to present a bait on a much lighter and smaller float tackle.

Generally speaking, only two basic types of float are required: a large one which will carry several swan shot and a smaller one to carry small shot in the No 3 to dust-shot range. Swan quills, goose quills, porcupines or floats made from cane and balsa wood are essential for fishing the deep strong-flowing swims and the smaller quills, or floats made from cane and balsa wood, for fishing the slow-moving swims. These are available in many different sizes and a selection of them should meet all likely requirements. Antenna floats are not often used because the thin tip is difficult to see at long range.

The colour of the float tip is quite important. Red and scarlet are useful colours in any light. Yellow and orange reflect more light and are easier to see when the sun is behind the angler and shining downstream. Black and red colours are easier to see when the water has a bright, silvery sheen.

Hooks, either eyed or spade-end, in sizes from 4 to 16 complete the tackle requirements. The smallest hooks are rarely required unless a maggot or caster is being used as bait.

METHODS

Float fishing for chub means long-trotting which, as the term implies, entails using a float to carry a bait long distances downstream; laying-on and float-legering, in which the bait is fished on the bottom; stret-pegging, which is a method used to work a float-fished bait downstream on the bottom by lifting and lowering the rod; and holding-on, in which the float is held on a tight line close under the rod tip with the weight so attached as to keep the bait off the bottom. Most of these methods are in common use and well-known to the majority of coarse fishermen.

ADAPTING METHODS TO SWIMS

Most rivers contain a number of deep swims and though their depth, size and the strength of the current may vary, they are basically similar in character. They often hold many chub, especially during the winter, and if it is intended to fish them with a moving bait the long-trotting method is the one to use.

When the water is at or above normal level tackle needs are met with a 13ft rod, a large quill or balsa wood float and a fixed-spool reel loaded with line of at least 3lb breaking strain. Hook size depends very much upon the size of the bait used. For cheese, flake, lobworm, paste, or crust, all excellent baits to use for this style of fishing, a No 4 or 6 hook is not too big. For casters or maggots a No 14 or 16 is required.

The size of the float must be related to the strength of current and the depth of water. A large float is essential for fishing the deeper faster-flowing swims as small floats will not carry enough shot to get the bait down through the powerful currents. Use a swan quill or a cane and balsa wood float that will carry several swan shot.

The depth at which the float is set depends upon the feeding depth of the chub. Normally, this will be at a point closer to the bottom than the surface, so it is best to set the depth at below mid-water level and then to deepen it gradually until the correct feeding depth is located.

If the chub are lying close to the bottom the bait must be made to sink quickly, which means that the bulk of the weights must be placed closer to the hook than to the float, otherwise the bait will not get down to the chub. A slower sinking effect is achieved by spacing the weights out up the cast, the smallest shot being placed closest to the hook.

The common practice of attaching split-shot directly to the line can seriously weaken the line through compression and it is better to attach the shot to a separate link or to thread drilled shot directly on to the line and use just one small shot as a stop. Even this shot can be dispensed with if a rubber stop is used instead. (See Fig 9.)

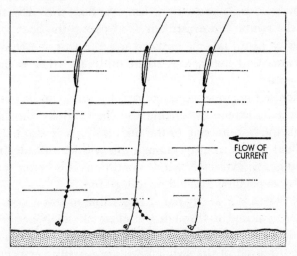

FLOW OF CURRENT

Fig 9   Three different tackles for float fishing in rivers

This method of attaching the weight greatly reduces the risk of line breakage and the tackle can be quickly converted to a float-legering style by altering the depth at which the float is set. As a further aid to quick tackle change the float should be attached to the line by two rubber rings so that it can be removed and replaced as required.

If the water is very clear and the chub can be seen the float should be carefully guided down the swim to where they are shoaling. If they are invisible the angler will have to use the knowledge he has acquired of each swim to determine where they are most likely to be in the prevailing conditions. Each swim is different but the angler who really knows his river will usually have a shrewd idea as to where the chub are most likely to be.

Ideal conditions for long-trotting are when the water is at normal level or fining down after a spate, the day windless and the sun veiled by cloud. More often, however, it is far from windless and a side wind will cause a 'bellying' of the line which must be 'mended' constantly to keep the float travelling steadily down the swim. A downstream wind causes the float to travel at a faster rate than the current and the bait to behave in a jerky unnatural manner. A slight upstream wind is the least troublesome.

Difficulties in presentation caused by wind can be overcome to a certain extent by sinking the line and by threading it through the bottom ring of the float only. It is also helpful to use a float with a thin tip, though this will be difficult to see at long range. In extremely windy conditions it is better to revert to the stret-pegging method or to legering.

If the swim is a weedy one it is possible to trot a float tackle down by guiding it through the clear channels between the weeds but the stret-pegging method allows a slower and more thorough search of the swim. Bites are usually very emphatic so a strong line is essential. A lobworm is the best bait when the water is coloured; cheese, paste or crust when the water is clear.

If the weeds are such that they cover the bottom of the swim entirely the tackle must be adjusted to keep the bait above the weeds. In the slower-moving stretches of some rivers there are often beds of lilies, sometimes termed 'cabbage-patches', which can only be fished in this way or with a floating bait. They often hold chub though and should not be passed over merely because they look difficult.

CLOSE-RANGE METHODS

It is often possible to catch chub at close range, even right under the rod tip, in which case both float visibility and bite detection become much easier. The particular method used naturally depends greatly on the nature of the swim and most of those in which close-range methods can be effective are relatively small and sometimes complicated by snags or overgrowth of bushes or trees.

Some swims are difficult, even impossible, to fish with a leger or a moving bait, either because the river bed is littered with rocks or other snags or because overhanging branches prevent the free passage of a float tackle. Both difficulties are sometimes encountered and the best way to overcome them is to use the holding-on style. This method ensures that the bait is held up above the snags and also allows it to be fished under the overhangs while the float itself is held on a tight line clear of the overhangs. (See Fig 10.)

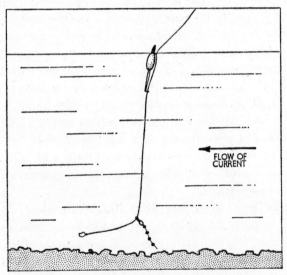

Fig 10   Tackle for fishing a snaggy bottom

It is also a useful method for fishing those areas of swirling currents that are common in most rivers, only in this case the float is not held on a tight line but allowed to circulate freely with the current. It is particularly suitable for fishing the slacks when the water is high and coloured and the surface littered with drifting debris.

Small Pools and Shallow Swims

No swim or pool should be neglected however small and so long as there is sufficient depth of water, or a weed-bed, overhang or undercut under which chub can hide, the swim should be tried either with the laying-on style or with a float-leger.

Both methods can be fished downstream or upstream, as required. If there is sufficient cover at the upstream end of the swim the downstream style can be safely used. If not, it is a wiser tactic to fish the tackle upstream from a position at the downstream end of the swim.

In some swims the current will pull the float under but this does not matter because as soon as the chub picks up the bait the float will rise to the surface giving a positive and easily detected bite indication. Alternatively, a closer approach will allow the float to be pulled up above the water where it is not affected by the current. The bite is registered in a similar way when the line falls slack and the float swings back downstream. A small streamlined float is best for this style of fishing.

Swimming a bait downstream on a float tackle seems such a natural form of presentation that few anglers reverse the procedure, yet fishing a float tackle upstream will often catch chub from swims in which the normal downstream style is difficult or impossible.

Shallow clear swims and those fringed by dense masses of reeds are typical examples of swims which are best fished in this way. And if it is necessary to wade out into the river to gain a good casting position there is no reason why this should not be done so long as it is done carefully and quietly.

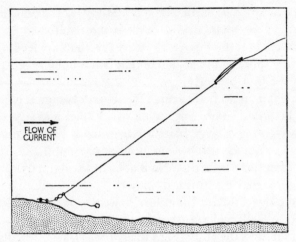

Fig 11   Upstream legering tackle

The float is set at a depth which will allow the bait to drift back downstream clear of the bottom and cast upstream with a gentle, underhand swinging movement. Line is then reeled in to keep in touch with the float as it falls back but at no time should the line pull on the float or the chub are likely to be alarmed by so unnatural a movement. The style, in fact, is very similar to that of upstream worming, except that a float is used in conjunction with a longer rod. (See Fig 11.)

All float-fishing methods can be used in weir-pools where many different variations in current and depth are to be found. It is also quite possible to float-fish a bait upstream, either on or off bottom, and there are often places where a counter-current can be used to drift the bait back upstream towards the sill. A large float and plenty of shot are usually needed to get the bait down against the strong currents.

POINTERS TO SUCCESS

Methods alone do not guarantee success so do not stick

slavishly to any one particular style. Study each swim carefully
and choose the method you think is most suited to it. Make
sure the bait is getting down to where the chub are feeding; it is
a common mistake to use tackle that is too lightly-weighted to
present the bait properly.

If a big float is needed to carry the required amount of weight,
do not be afraid to use one. Avoid weak lines and small hooks
when presenting a large bait; a No 16 hook may be fine for a
maggot but not for a lobworm, a large piece of flake, crust, or
cheese. Fish these baits on a No 8 hook at least and use a strong
line, 4–6lb breaking strain, to match.

Some anglers advise the use of a weaker hook link—a 1½lb
link tied to a 3lb reel line or some similar arrangement—on the
assumption that the chub is less likely to see the minimally finer
line or that, in some way, it improves bait presentation. I do
not agree and though such an arrangement does have the
advantage of losing only the link if the tackle should get
snagged up I still think it is safer and just as effective to use line
of the same strength throughout from reel to hook.

Admittedly, there are times—usually when the water is very
clear—when chub do become wary of tackle or the way in
which the bait is presented. If so, a change to a finer line and
a smaller hook should be tried but, normally, chub can be
caught in almost any situation on lines of between 3–8lb breaking-strain depending upon conditions and the nature of the
swim. The best policy, then, is to start off with strong tackle
and to scale it down only when there is good reason—and there
could be many others—to believe that it is responsible for any
lack of sport. Even if there are snags or thick weed-beds in the
swim it is still wiser to persist with the stronger tackle since there
is no point in hooking a chub only to lose it through an avoid-
able breakage.

If groundbait is used in conjunction with a float-fishing style—
as it often is—the style of presentation and the pattern of
groundbaiting should be closely related. If a heavy groundbait

is used the bait must be fished deep, too. If, on the other hand, the groundbait is of the light slow-sinking variety then a slow-sinking style of presentation should also be used for the hook bait.

Always try to keep the float travelling down that part of the swim where the groundbait has been thrown in and do not throw it in immediately you arrive at a swim but try it first with the baited tackle. I have lost count now of the number of chub I have caught by adopting this simple ploy.

8

Still Waters and Canals

Chub are found in shallow weedy ponds, large lakes, gravel-pits and in some reservoirs. Their feeding habits obviously vary in these different waters, chub in waters deficient in natural foods being comparatively easy to catch while those in waters rich in natural foods are more wary. It is also true that waters containing an abundance of food organisms not only often produce more chub than the food-deficient waters but usually produce larger ones, too.

Singling chub out from other competing species in such waters may seem difficult, if not impossible. It is certainly more difficult than in rivers but it can be done if the basic principles of first locating them and then fishing for them with a bait they are most likely to take are followed. In the summer they can sometimes be seen rising to take insects from the surface. It is also possible to find them feeding in and around the weed-beds. When they cannot be seen, patient and systematic exploration of the water with a selective bait will often help to locate a feeding shoal.

All tackle needs can be met with the same equipment as for river fishing: a legering rod, a float-fishing rod at least 12ft long, a fly-fishing rod and a spinning rod. Other useful items are a few bubble-floats in various sizes, a selection of weighted self-cocking floats and a few sliding floats.

CLOSE-RANGE METHODS

Some still waters are very clear and as there is no perceptible current, unless a strong wind is blowing, it is not possible to know which way the chub are facing. This obviously makes it more difficult to make an unobserved approach, and is the reason why it is essential to move quietly and to take advantage of any available cover.

Fishing The Margins

One of the most enjoyable methods of catching still-water chub is to take rod and bait and embark on a systematic exploration of the margins of the water, casting and retrieving the bait in the hope of contacting a feeding chub. This method is really an adaptation of the hunting method previously described to the needs of still-water fishing. The same tackle, consisting of legering rod, fixed-spool reel loaded with line of at least 4lb breaking-strain, and a No 4 hook baited with a lobworm, is ideal. No float or weight is needed, the weight of the worm being sufficient to make casting easy. Long casting is not necessary except in those waters which have extensive shallows or weedy margins.

As when river fishing, dawn and dusk are the best times to use this style of fishing; dawn, when the water is undisturbed, being perhaps the best time of all. During the day a strong, warm inshore wind which breaks up the surface and encourages the chub to move inshore also increases the chances of success.

To employ the method successfully the first cast should be made straight out from the bank and the worm allowed to sink. When it has reached bottom it should be retrieved either in a sink-and-draw style or by working it along the bottom in a series of slow pulling movements, all the time slowly reeling in the slack line. When the worm has been worked into the shore a fresh cast should be made at a different angle. Each cast should then be similarly advanced until the immediate area has been thoroughly covered.

The same tactics are used to fish with a minnow but this bait

F

is best fished on a float tackle which will sink it quickly through the surface water yet prevent it from hiding in the bottom weed-growth. Ideally, the float should be just buoyant enough to prevent the minnow from dragging it under and the moment the float disappears the strike should be made.

A float attached in the normal way, using both rings, will serve for shallow-water fishing but a sliding float is essential for deep water. It should be threaded onto the line and two stops attached: one above the float to mark the maximum depth to which the minnow bait will sink and the other below the float, about a yard from the hook. A weight is then attached about half-way between the bottom stop and the hook. In windy conditions it is preferable to use a float attached by its bottom ring only and to sink the line. (See Fig 12.)

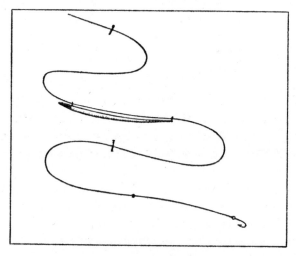

Fig 12   Sliding-float tackle

Static Methods

If the presence of other anglers makes it necessary to remain in one particular swim it will be best to fish the bait on the bottom or in a slow-sinking style. If the bottom-fishing style is chosen the laying-on or float-legering method should be used. A fixed float is suitable for fishing shallow water but a sliding float is preferable for deep water. The stops are attached as previously explained but the top stop should be tied on at a greater depth than that of the water and the bottom weight attached closer to the hook. A split-shot is used for the laying-on method and a small leger weight for float-legering. (See Fig 13.)

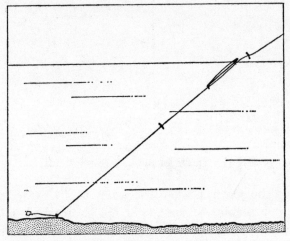

Fig 13   Float-leger tackle

A reasonably strong line should be used for this style of fishing—3lb at least. Chub are not as formidable a proposition in still waters as they are in overgrown rivers but, even so, it would be unwise to fish with a weak line. For fishing weedy swims a strong line is essential and a 6lb breaking strain would not be too strong for some swims.

When the bottom is covered by a dense weed growth it is essential that the bait remains visible and one way of ensuring this is to use a large piece of crust or flake which will rest on top of the weed. Another way is to set the depth at which the bait is fished so precisely that the bait remains just above the weeds.

This is essential if a worm is used, otherwise it will burrow into the weed and become invisible. (See Fig 14.)

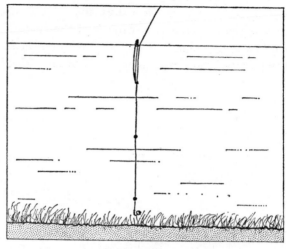

Fig 14   Tackle for fishing a weedy bottom

During the summer when the water is often calm a slow-sinking style should be used to tempt chub which might be cruising at mid-water level or even just under the surface. Baits such as a lobworm or a piece of cheese can be presented on weightless tackle. Other baits should be weighted sufficiently to sink them very slowly.

Both the fixed float and the sliding float styles can be used to present the bait. A sliding float is essential for deep water but the fixed float is quite satisfactory for shallow-water fishing. Baits fished in this close-range, slow-sinking style can be very effective at times, providing the angler remains quiet and concealed, and reed-beds in particular are often favourite hiding places for chub and well worth exploring.

Legering

When the water is rough float-fishing is still possible but bite detection becomes difficult and it is then advisable to switch to legering. The bait is less likely to be pulled out of position and bites are usually easy to detect. The amount of weight used will obviously vary according to the conditions. A swan shot or a $\frac{1}{4}$–$\frac{1}{2}$oz leger weight should meet all requirements for close-range legering.

Once the bait has been cast out and has settled in position the rod should be placed in a rest and a loop of slack line allowed to form between rod tip and the surface which will tighten when a chub picks up the bait. A bite indicator can be used if desired, the swing-tip being very useful for still-water legering.

The Rolling Leger

This method is not usually associated with still-water fishing but strong winds often create an undercurrent which flows in the opposite direction to the surface current. In these conditions difficulty may be experienced in holding the weight in one place and it is then that the rolling leger can be used to cover the swim in a series of wide sweeping arcs. The technique used is similar to that used in rivers, the cast being progressively advanced to cover as much water as possible. A lobworm, cheese or a minnow are all excellent baits to use under these conditions.

LONG-RANGE METHODS

It is a common fallacy that the best fish always lie a long way out from the bank. Strong inshore winds often bring the chub into the margins and it is only when the wind drops that they tend to retreat outwards and away from the banks. This movement is most marked in waters which have shallow margins, when the sun is full on the water, and when the banks are crowded with anglers. A combination of any of these factors considerably reduces the chances of catching chub from the margins and it is then that long-casting methods are often required.

For long-distance float fishing a rod at least 12ft long, a 3–4lb line and a weighted sliding float will be needed. With this tackle it is possible to cast much further than with an ordinary float and at the same time to use a slow-sinking method of presentation because most of the required weight is contained within the float. The tackle set-up is the same as that illustrated in Figure 13 and the best baits are cheese or lob-worm, both of which will withstand the effects of casting better than the soft bread baits.

For long-distance legering the requirements are a 10–11ft legering rod, 4–6lb line and a selection of weights up to 1oz. A well-filled spool is also necessary for smooth efficient casting. Once the baited tackle has been cast out it can be left in the same position for a long time or withdrawn and re-cast at intervals to cover a larger area of water. Either is capable of producing good results but success is obviously more likely if the chub have first been accurately located.

SURFACE FISHING

During the summer a floating crust will sometimes lure a surface feeding chub but a favourable offshore wind or a current from a feeder stream will be needed to drift the bait out any distance. A large piece of crust is impaled on a No 4 hook, tied to a 6lb line and allowed to drift out to where the chub are rising. No float is needed and the strong tackle is essential to withstand the strain of hooking a chub at long range.

Live flies and chrysalids will also sometimes tempt surface-feeding chub but it is then necessary to use a float and a smaller hook, a No 12 or 14. The longer and more flexible rod, a 4lb line and a bubble float or small loaded float make an ideal combination for this style.

CANALS

Comparatively few anglers fish for chub in canals although they are more common in such waters than is generally thought.

Even so, locating chub in canals can be a daunting task. During the summer they can sometimes be seen lying over or between submerged weeds or rising to take insects from the surface. But for the most part they remain invisible and can only be located by a systematic exploration of all likely swims, aided perhaps by a prebaiting with a favourite chub bait such as cheese or lobworm.

Any parts of a canal bordered by overhanging trees or bushes and fast-flowing swims below lock-gates should be given special attention as these can be favourite places in the summer because of the high oxygen content of the water. A further aid to location can be a study of the formation of the canal bed. Most canals are deepest in their centre channel, often known as the 'boat road', whereas others are deeper under the far bank. Normally, chub lie in or close to the deeper water and will not be attracted to the shallow parts of a canal during daylight hours, unless they are hunting fry or minnows. When the sun is full on the water they often shelter in the shade of the thick weed-beds and lilies have a special attraction for them.

METHODS

Most of the methods, tackle and baits used to catch chub in rivers and still waters can also be used for canal fishing. The traditional fine-and-far-off style of the canal angler will some-times catch chub but there is ample scope as well for more imaginative styles of fishing such as hunting, legering, surface-fishing and fly-fishing.

The hunting method is most effective when chub can actually be seen in the canal, or when the angler knows where to locate them. The same tackle as used for hunting in rivers—10ft legering rod, 4–6lb line and a large hook baited with minnow, lobworm, cheese or bread—should be used and the best times are early morning or evening when the banks are more likely to be free of other anglers and boat traffic less frequent.

Weedy stretches of the canal and the fast-flowing swims below lock-gates usually offer the best chance of catching chub with this style of fishing. The bait is cast or lowered into every accessible space between the weeds and allowed to remain there for a few minutes before being withdrawn. There may be a quick take though more often patient and persistent effort is required before any results are obtained. The slower moving, weedless parts of the canal should be fished with particular care and always upstream.

Both upstream and downstream legering methods can be used to catch canal chub. Downstream legering is possible wherever there is sufficient cover in the form of reed-beds or other bankside growth, but where there is no cover and the water is very clear it is wiser to leger upstream. Strong tackle is essential for fishing the weedy swims and the fast water below lock-gates but finer line and less weight can be used in the clearer stretches provided it is matched with a more flexible rod. Never try to compromise on this issue. On balance it is better to use the stronger tackle in most swims as it permits a firmer strike and considerably lessens the risk of the chub escaping.

Under-the-rod-tip legering, with or without a float, is another method that can be adapted to canal fishing and though a longer rod for fishing those clear swims beyond the reach of the legering rod can be useful it is not essential.

Float-fishing methods are obviously best suited to the clear deep parts of the canal, the slow-sinking style being the most popular for any species of fish. If a lobworm or cheese bait is used additional weight will not be needed, but the natural buoyancy of crust or flake will have to be compensated for by the addition of weights.

A 12–13ft rod and a 2–3lb line should be strong enough to handle most chub caught in clear water but stronger tackle is advisable if there are weed-beds close by. If the depth of the float is set so that the bait just clears the bottom at maximum fall, this tackle can be used to search downstream over many yards of water, just as it can in rivers.

Among the several methods which can be used to fish at close range one is to hold the bait on a tight line under the rod tip with the shot concentrated to keep the bait off the bottom as in Figure 10. This is ideal for holding the bait in a restricted swim or off a weeded bottom in a strong current. Where the current is negligible the tackle should be adjusted to keep the bait above the weed or just resting on it as in Figure 14.

Clean swims present few problems. The bait is fished on the bottom either by the laying-on or float-legering method and in windy conditions an antenna float attached by its bottom ring only is to be recommended.

The methods of fishing a live fly, chrysalid or crust on the surface described in previous chapters can also be used in canals. The quieter periods when boat traffic and other anglers are not disturbing the water are more likely to be productive, evening times being possibly the best of all.

9

Still-water Fly Fishing

Fly fishing is possibly the most interesting and to some extent the most selective method of catching chub in still waters, though rarely used by coarse-fish anglers in search of other quarries.

Undoubtedly the best results are obtained during the summer when insect life is most prolific and when chub are more likely to be feeding along the margins. Early morning and evening are the best times but chub can be caught throughout the day providing there is not too much noise on the banks or disturbance of the water. A strong onshore breeze also increases one's chances and for this reason it is good angling tactics to fish into the wind. Casting may be more difficult but the results gained, especially with the deeply sunken wet fly or nymph, make the effort worthwhile.

Obviously, if a fishery contains other coarse fish, and possibly trout as well, species other than chub are likely to be caught. In such cases a knowledge of the water and of the most likely places where his particular quarry is to be found will be invaluable to the chub hunter.

TACKLE

The equipment used for fly fishing in rivers is usually equally suitable for still-water fly fishing but if it is necessary to cast long distances a fibreglass rod, 8–9ft long, which can be as light as 4oz yet powerful enough to cast a long line, will be required.

With this type of rod and using the shooting-head system—
which is rigged up by splicing a length of fly line to a backing of
nylon or braided line—and the double-haul style of casting it is
possible to make much longer casts than with a rod intended
only for river fishing.

Such a rod is most useful in waters with extensive shallow
margins and carefully-trimmed banks which allow manipula-
tion of the line without fear of snagging on the back cast. Such
ideal conditions are not, however, to be found in every still
water and where the marginal water is deep and the banks high
and overgrown a 10ft rod is more likely to keep the line clear of
the high banks on the back cast.

For leaders, the tapered variety are best for the delicate
presentation needed with the dry fly, whereas a leader of uniform strength throughout can be used for wet-fly and nymph
fishing. Shorter leaders with a steeper taper are required for
casting into the wind but as a general rule it would be unwise to
use a leader with a point of less than 3lb breaking-strain.

NATURAL FLIES AND THEIR IMITATIONS

Many different flies and insects are found in and around most
still waters, the most important to the angler being the sedgefly,
mayfly, lake olive, alder fly and hawthorn fly, cranefly, midge,
flying ant, gnat, dragonfly and damselfly as well as various
types of beetle. The beetles belong to two specific groups: those
that live underwater, such as the Dytiscus, and the land-based
beetles which include the cockchafer and soldier beetles.

Imitations of these flies, their nymphs and the beetles should
therefore form the nucleus of any selection of flies intended for
catching chub from still waters. Thus a dry-fly selection would
include such artificials as the Mayfly, Lake Olive, Hawthorn
Fly, Alder Fly, Black Gnat, Daddy-long-legs, Dragonfly and
Damselfly, together with a few sedge patterns of which my
favourite is the Cinnamon Sedge. I would also include those

two firm favourites, Wickham's Fancy and Greenwell's Glory and, to imitate the beetles, Cochybondhu, Hoolet and Cockchafer. Many other patterns could be added to the list but those named should adequately meet most needs.

CHOOSING THE FLY

Chub will not rise unless there is a natural insect or a convincing imitation of one on the water. The natural may be a hatching fly or an insect that has fallen into the water and the first step is to try to identify the insect the chub are feeding on and to match it with an imitation.

The most difficult choice to be made is when chub are feeding on the tiny midges that get bogged down in the surface film and are almost invisible to the human eye. In this case, a midge imitation, Black Gnat, Green Midge or perhaps a Black Ant should be tried. Chub do not in my experience show much discrimination as regards the pattern of fly used but they do sometimes prefer very small flies to the larger ones. It is therefore logical to start by using a small fly when the chub are actually feeding on them and the fact that they will sometimes also take a larger Greenwell's Glory or Lake Olive does not invalidate the reasoning.

When the water is very clear the larger Sedges, Daddy-longlegs, Dragonflies and Moths are most likely to produce results in the evening when the light is fading and also when there are some natural flies on the water. Wind will sometimes carry the land-based flies and insects onto the water and in these conditions the Alder, Hawthorn or Sedgefly imitations are always worth trying.

In the absence of any rise, the dry fly is still worth a trial, especially in the shallower lakes where anything that alights on the surface is more easily discerned and taken. But in most cases the lack of any rises means that the chub are feeding on the bottom and a change to wet fly or nymph is then indicated.

PRESENTING THE DRY FLY

There are several ways of fishing the dry fly in still waters. One is to look for a rising chub and to cast a fly as near to the rise as possible. Great care is needed if this method is to be used successfully, and it is advisable not to get too close unless there is some cover to screen your approach. For the most delicate presentation during daylight and when the sun is full on the water a leader at least 9ft long is advisable. Casting movements should be kept down to a minimum as too many unnecessary false casts will quickly put the chub down.

Another way of fishing the dry fly is to work slowly and quietly around the margins, always casting the fly ahead into undisturbed water in the hope that it will be seen by a feeding chub. This method is most likely to get results when there is an inshore breeze in the early morning or at dusk when the chub are probably feeding close in to the shore.

It is not necessary to make long casts and when casting is difficult because of high banks it is best to fish so that the casting arm is on that side of the body which is turned away from the bank. The risk of the leader or fly getting snarled up on the back cast is then much reduced and if the same length of the cast is maintained it is possible to withdraw and re-cast in one easy movement, and so progress comfortably and methodically around the margins.

Long-distance casting is difficult if not impossible if one is hampered by high overgrown banks and is in any event unnecessary on the majority of still waters. Most of the chub I have caught have been taken at less than twenty yards range. If however, the margins are shallow, long casting may sometimes be necessary in order to reach chub that are rising well beyond normal casting range, in which case it will be necessary to discard the tackle used for margin fishing in favour of the shooting-head line. Both casting and striking become more difficult as the length of the cast increases though, so the method should be used only when it is essential and not from force of habit or merely to demonstrate a superior casting ability.

An offshore breeze permits the use of yet another method, sometimes known as blow-lining but more correctly as dapping. The 10ft rod with light double-taper line and a long tapered leader should be used. The fly should have plenty of hackle to catch the wind and should be perfectly dry. One of the sedge-flies or an Alder, Hawthorn, Dragonfly or even a Mayfly can be used and the line should of course float as a sinking line will hinder both presentation and striking efficiency. One of the modern air-cell lines is ideal.

To present the fly the rod is held up to the fullest extent of the arm so that the wind will carry the fly out over the water where it is allowed to fall by gradually lowering the arm until the fly alights softly on the surface. A boat permits more water to be covered, but the method can be used quite successfully from the shore.

Fishing a dry fly into the wind can sometimes be rewarding and is not too difficult if a shorter leader is used and more power put into the forward cast to cut the line sharply through the wind. I often use a level 6lb leader only 6ft long, and an even shorter one in very strong winds.

WET FLIES AND LURES

Patterns of wet fly are just as numerous as dry-fly patterns and one should try to narrow down one's selection to those flies which experience has shown are most likely to tempt chub. It should certainly include most if not all of the following: Silver Butcher, Bloody Butcher, Zulu, Alder, Hawthorn, Invicta, Peter Ross, Alexandra, Mayfly and Greenwell's Glory. There are many others and if a selection of the numerous available lures and streamers were to be included the list could be extended considerably.

The best course to adopt with lures is to give an extended trial to just a few selected patterns rather than constantly switch from one to the other in an effort to find the ideal one. The Polystickle should be regarded as essential, and Sinfoil's Fry, Dunkeld, Black Lure, Yellow Perch, Grey Ghost, Jersey Herd and the Muddler Minnow should also be tried. The Polystickle is a noted chub killer and the Muddler Minnow resembles a bullhead, upon which chub feed as avidly as on minnows when they are available. A special weedless wet fly is also available for fishing in weedy swims.

PRESENTING THE WET FLY

Wet-fly fishing is often more rewarding than dry-fly fishing, though much depends upon the feeding habits of the chub and the amount of time and patience that is devoted to casting and working the flies. Two or three flies are used as required: one on the point and the others on droppers and it is helpful, though not essential, to use a leader that is approximately as long as the water is deep. One can then judge when the point fly has reached bottom merely by allowing all the leader to sink beneath the surface.

This method of relating leader length to depth cannot be used in very deep water as the length of the leader would make close-range casting difficult, if not impossible. The extra depth has therefore to be attained by using a sinking line and these, like other lines, are available in different sizes and even at different sinking speeds. For close-range work in relatively shallow water a forward taper sinking line and a leader linked to depth will suffice, but for long-range work in deep water it will be necessary to revert to the shooting-head system and a sinking line.

Wet flies should be presented in the same manner as dry flies—by working carefully and methodically along the margins, covering each area thoroughly before moving on. The most obvious difference is the absence of any rise, the wet-fly method being very much of a probing and searching operation designed to seek out chub feeding in the lower strata of the water.

There are several recommended methods of working the flies. One is to allow them to sink to the fullest extent of the leader and then withdraw them in a rapid zig-zag manner. Since the object is to imitate darting fry, flies with a glint of silver on their bodies such as the Silver or Bloody Butcher, or the Zulu, are excellent ones to use. A strong leader of at least 4lb breaking-strain should be used as chub often snap at the flies while they are moving and if the leader is not strong enough both fish and flies will be lost.

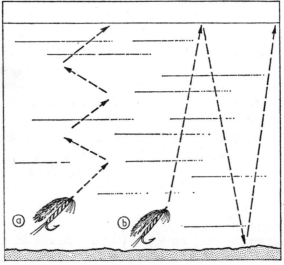

Fig 15   Two methods of fishing a wet fly or lure

Another method is to allow the fly to sink to the bottom and then work it very slowly in towards the bank in imitation of a small fish grubbing along the bottom. This method is worth trying on those cold days when no fish are showing and prospects seem generally unfavourable. One fly on the point will suffice, the Muddler Minnow and Polystickle being favourites for this style of fishing. (See Fig 15.)

Two or even three flies can be used for the sink-and-draw style. The flies are first cast out, allowed to sink and then worked gradually into the bank by lifting and lowering the rod tip, the final withdrawal being made right under the rod tip. The cast is then repeated to cover a fresh area of water and the sink-and-draw process repeated. A take sometimes occurs while the flies are sinking but is more likely to occur while they are being withdrawn.

NYMPHS AND OTHER IMITATIONS

Nymphs are an important part of the diet of all fish and are usually present in large numbers in any still water, though their number and variety naturally varies according to the location and nature of the water. Those most likely to be found in still waters are nymphs of the lake olive, alderfly, mayfly, damselfly, dragonfly and the chironomids or midges. Other forms of life such as beetles, shrimps and snails are also found in most still waters.

Most of the chub I have caught have fallen to such artificials as a Lake Olive nymph, Pheasant Tail nymph, Dragonfly nymph and, rather surprisingly, the March Brown nymph. I have also had some success with others and would advise the inclusion of the Damselfly nymph, Alderfly nymph, Amber nymph, Geoffrey Bucknall's Footballer (or other imitation midge pupae) Richard Walker's Chomper and Barney Google, the Caddis or Sedge pupa and the Corixa.

PRESENTING THE NYMPH

When the chub are feeding deep the artificial should be

G

fished deep, too. I prefer to use only one nymph tied to the point of the leader. This is cast out, allowed to sink and then worked gradually back to the bank in a series of jerking motions imitative of the swimming movements of the live nymph. These movements are quite easy to imitate. The rod is held low, parallel to the bank, and line is gathered in with the left hand while the rod is moved in a regular but gentle jerking motion. The aim is to keep the nymph close to the bottom where the chub expect to find it and to give it lifelike movement.

When the nymph has been worked inshore it should be lifted slowly to the surface and as this movement corresponds to the rise of the hatching nymph it is not unusual for the chub to hook itself if it takes the nymph at this stage. If however the nymph is seized while it is sinking the take is seen rather than felt, and a close watch should be kept on the line for any unnatural quickening in the rate of descent. An alternative way of fishing the nymph is to rest it for a few seconds between each swimming movement. This is a particularly effective way of fishing a shrimp or beetle imitation.

Caddis grubs should normally be fished very slowly and deep but if chub are rising to take nymphs from just beneath the surface the nymph should be fished hanging at the same level. The leader is greased to ensure that it will float and the nymph cast out so that it will drift slowly round into the feeding area. A slight breeze is helpful as it carries the nymphs round on a broad drift and also imparts movement to them. I find it more productive of results to drift the nymphs in this way rather than cast them directly to where the chub are feeding. This tactic may sometimes produce results but the fish are more likely to be scared by the impact of line and leader on the water, especially in bright sunny conditions. (See Fig 16.)

Two or even three nymphs can be used for this style of fishing and a take is usually signified by a slight swirl followed by the leader and line streaking away in an unmistakable manner. Tighten quickly and then hold on. Unless there are weed-beds nearby the chub should be mastered and brought to the net without too much trouble.

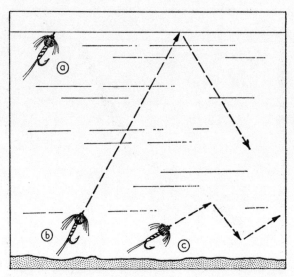

Fig 16   Three methods of fishing a nymph in still water

OTHER METHODS

Lack of proper fly-fishing equipment should not deter any angler from trying this fascinating method of catching chub as close-range fishing with dry fly, wet fly or nymph are all possible with a coarse-fishing rod and a nylon line. The dry fly can be dapped, as previously described and it is only necessary to add a small split shot to the leader to sink the wet fly or nymph.

Long-range fishing can be done in several ways. One is to attach a large bushy fly to the line and to make use of an off-shore wind to drift it out to where the chub are rising. Another method is to use a bubble-float or a loaded float. These methods may not appeal to purists and certainly should not be tried when local rules prohibit their use, but where they are considered legitimate they are well worth trying, if only as an introduction to the real thing. (See Fig 17.)

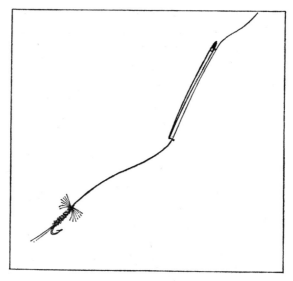

Fig 17   Float tackle for fly fishing

CANALS

Very few anglers attempt to catch chub from canals with an artificial fly or nymph but the idea should not be lightly dismissed and if chub can be seen rising to take flies from the surface a carefully cast artificial will sometimes tempt them.

Most patterns of fly already mentioned could be used, the smaller ones being preferred when the chub are feeding on small flies and when the sun is full on the water. At dusk a White Moth, Alder, Hawthorn or one of the sedgeflies should be tried. Imitations of damselflies and dragonflies are also worth a trial as both are common along the banks of many canals.

Wet-fly and nymph-fishing are not as effective in canals as on still waters, especially in the summer when there is a prolific weed-growth in most canals but where this is only slight both methods can be used. Great care must be exercised in the approach though as once scared chub are exceedingly difficult to tempt and it is best to fish up the canal, casting the fly up and across as one does when river fishing.

The summer and autumn months offer the best chance of catching chub on the fly. During the winter they seldom rise, except perhaps for a brief period at dusk, and other methods are more effective.

10

In Search of Specimens

In his book published in 1879 the Rev Houghton wrote: 'A chub of 3–4lb could be considered a good fish. Yarrell says that one of 5lb is the most he can find recorded.' Cholmondeley Pennel, another angling writer of the same period, disagreed, and gave details of some splendid chub. One of these weighed 5lb 5½oz and measured 21in. Another weighed 6lb 2½oz and measured 22in. The best weighed 7lb ½oz and measured 23in.

William Bailey thought that the river Trent offered the best chub fishing in the land, as this extract from his book *The Angler's Instructor* reveals:

> We think nothing of a chub 4lb in weight. I killed one once that was only 2oz under 7lb. This was the largest I ever saw but 5–6 pounders are very common in the Trent. I have several friends who come from London for a few days fishing and they say that the Trent chub are the largest they have ever seen.

A much larger chub, weighing 8lb was taken from the Trent by a Newark angler towards the close of the nineteenth century.

H. T. Sheringham, author of *An Angler's Hours* published in 1902, thought the river Thames was a splendid river for chub. 'It would be hard to find its equal,' he wrote. 'I know of a quiet corner, where in a clear spot between the rushes, lie some chub of astonishing magnitude. Two of them are certainly the better part of a yard long.'

He also knew of other rivers where chub weighing between 4 and 5lb could be seen basking on the surface. The Great Ouse, which has always been noted for the quality of its chub fishing, he thought particularly good. 'The river is full of big chub,' he wrote. 'In the neighbourhood of St Ives, where most of the river is free, many really large chub are caught every summer.'

Pollution has ruined some of Britain's once great rivers but many fine chub have been caught in post-war years. The record-holder—until it was disqualified—was the 10½lb chub caught with a fly from the river Annan in 1955 by Dr Cameron. This chub was caught accidentally and was not properly authenticated. It equalled in weight another monster caught from the river Crane in Middlesex by a Mr Cockburn in 1875. This chub took a float-fished minnow.

For many years, from 1913 until 1951, an 8lb 4oz chub caught from the Hampshire Avon by G. F. Smith held the record but in 1951 this fish was bettered by one of 8lb 8oz caught from the Sussex Rother by Mr D. Deekes. Colonel John Byng, a gentleman of leisure who, in the eighteenth century travelled the country on horseback in pursuit of his favourite sport also sought chub in the Ouse. 'This morning,' he wrote in his diary, 'I realised my hopes by catching several fine chubs from the Ouse, several of which made my small rod to crack.'

The Hampshire Avon has probably produced more big chub than any other river in the British Isles. Chub weighing 5lb are common and Bill Warren, renowned for his catches of Avon chub, landed over 200 chub exceeding this weight, including thirteen over 6lb and one magnificent specimen weighing 7lb 6oz, between 1952 and 1959. Many other chub over 6lb have been taken from this river, most of them coming from the Royalty fishery at Christchurch. Two of the largest weighed 7lb 14oz and 8lb respectively, the latter falling to a cheese bait.

Fine river though it undoubtedly is, the Hampshire Avon does not have a monopoly of large chub and there are several other excellent chub rivers in the south of England. The Dorset Stour, the Kennet, Beult, Ouse, and Wey have all produced some outstanding chub, one of the best reported in recent years being a 7lb 6oz specimen caught with a lobworm by a fifteen-year-old boy, B. Hill, from the river Kennet. His rod top was wrecked in the struggle to land this magnificent fish. Other specimens taken in the south include a 7lb 2oz chub taken from the river Wey with a redworm bait, and a 6lb chub lured from the river Beult with cheese.

The Dorsetshire Stour has produced some particularly fine chub, too, one of the best being a 7lb 14½oz fish taken on a fly. Others weighing 7lb 8oz, 7lb 3oz and many over 6lb have been taken on various baits. Some of these chub were caught with hempseed—a killing bait until it was banned in the mid-sixties.

The Bedfordshire Ouse, the river which Colonel John Byng enjoyed fishing so much, is rated by some as the best chub river in the British Isles. Richard Walker has caught many chub weighing over 6lb from the Ouse, and believes that there are chub of over 10lb yet to be caught in some British rivers. In support of this he says he has seen much larger chub in the Ouse than any he has caught and mentions one found dead and decayed on the river bank at Offord which measured 27in and weighed 8lb 2oz.

An even larger chub was found dead on the banks of the nearby river Cherwell. It weighed 9lb 2oz even though its head and part of one shoulder had been eaten away. Another monster weighing 9lb 3oz was found dead on the banks of the river Waveney in Suffolk, an area not generally considered very highly for its chub fishing. This same river yielded a magnificent 7lb 9oz chub to S. Maddox of Stowmarket, Suffolk, who lost his chance of claiming the chub record when he put the fish back into the river. He was enjoying what he called 'a pleasure trip' when he hooked the chub and says it took him fifteen minutes to land it on a 4lb line.

There were no chub in the Waveney until the Norfolk River Board introduced them from the river Wye in 1956 and the size reached by the dead fish mentioned, as well as the one caught by Mr Maddox, indicates that they have adapted well to their new habitat, and that it is now capable of producing chub to compare with those of the more renowned rivers of the south.

The river Thames, where Sheringham says he saw chub 'the better part of a yard long', holds chub of a good average size and occasionally produces a really big one. Peter Stone, the well-known Oxford angler-writer, says four-pounders are common and Frank Murgett, who has written a book about fishing the Thames, once caught one that weighed 7lb 11oz. It took a gudgeon bait intended for trout.

Both the Severn and the Wye contain large numbers of chub and though they are not as notable for the size of their chub as the Avon or Stour they have yielded chub up to and over 6lb and large catches in the 2–3lb bracket are frequently taken from these two rivers.

In the north the Swale and Derwent have produced most of the specimens. Many chub of over 6lb have been taken from the Swale, one of the best being a 7lb 2oz fish caught with cheese by Major Peacock. An even bigger specimen weighing 7lb 15oz was taken from the Derwent by Mr Minton who afterwards expressed some disappointment with the fight put up by this huge fish.

The river Hull has also produced some fine specimens, one of the largest, a six-pounder, falling to floating crust. Bread-flake lured another monster weighing 6lb 12oz from the river Ribble.

Other lesser known rivers and streams sometimes surprise everyone by producing a specimen, too. Five-pounders are not uncommon and occasionally chub of over 6lb are caught. Both the river Welland and the little river Thet in Norfolk have yielded chub of this quality.

Scotland and the Border counties have a few rivers which also contain really big chub although they are not often fished for. Reports from local anglers indicate that the river Annan, which produced the disputed record chub, contains other monster chub. One angler reported seeing what he first thought was a salmon but later identified as a chub—a huge fish which refused his fly and other offerings and presently swam slowly away. Authenticated captures of chub over 6lb have also been made from the river Liddle, a tributary of the Border Esk, and from the river Eden. In each case the angler was fishing for trout with a fly and the chub were accidental captures.

STILL-WATER SPECIMENS

Still waters have not produced as many specimens as the rivers but enough have been caught to indicate that, given favourable conditions, still-water chub can attain specimen size. Some of the largest of such chub caught in post-war years have been taken from gravel pits, one of the largest being a 7lb 2oz fish caught in a Gloucestershire gravel pit. Other specimens include a 6lb 7oz chub caught with bread-paste from a Lincolnshire pit and a 6lb 4oz chub which took a small perch fished in a Buckinghamshire pit.

An outlet to Hemphones reservoir in Yorkshire yielded an unexpected 6lb 12½oz chub to RAF recruit Ian Webb. This monster took a lobworm and surprised its captor who was not fishing specifically for chub. But even this specimen, notable though it was, must take second place to a magnificent 7lb 4oz chub taken with a double maggot bait from Healey Dam in Yorkshire, again by an angler who was fishing at random.

CANAL SPECIMENS

Really big chub are not often caught from canals though a fair number over 5lb have been recorded in post-war years, one of the biggest being a 6lb 5oz fish taken from the Basingstoke canal with legered cheese. Sid Taylor, its captor, caught another chub weighing 5lb on the same day and a little later his clubmate, Ron Pugh, captured a 5lb 9oz specimen with cheese bait.

Other specimen chub have been taken from the Kennet and Avon canal and the Trent and Mersey canal. Quite probably there are big chub in other canals as well but they are seldom caught because so very few anglers deliberately fish for them.

An analysis of the baits taken by fifty outstanding specimens all over 6lb reveals an interesting pattern of preference. Cheese, worms, bread-baits and maggots, accounted for the majority of them, twelve falling to cheese, ten to worms, ten to bread-baits, nine to maggots, two to luncheon meat, three to livebaits of various kinds, one to a seed-bait, one to a slug, two to a fly. This sample suggests that cheese is the outstanding bait, closely followed by worms, bread-baits and maggots, while other popular chub baits such as minnows, slugs and crayfish do not appear to be so successful with the really big ones.

No firm conclusion however can be drawn from this particular analysis since the number of anglers using the most popular baits on any given day would certainly be far greater than the number using other baits. If more anglers used the less popular baits the picture might be very different. Nonetheless, it does seem significant that of the specimens listed no less than nine fell to maggots, which are not highly rated as a chub bait. These included some truly great fish weighing 7lb 4oz, 7lb 2oz and 7lb ½oz. The largest of these chub succumbed to a bunch of four maggots, the 7lb 2oz fish to two maggots and the 7lb ½oz fish to a single maggot. Another interesting fact is that five of the nine chub caught with maggots came from the Hampshire Avon, the Royalty fishery providing three of them.

Undoubtedly the number of maggots thrown in as ground bait accounts to some extent for the number of specimen chub caught from the Royalty, and tends to confirm the belief that the prolonged use of maggots can result in 'conditioned feeding' and perhaps to some specimen chub being caught. Nevertheless, the maggot is too attractive to other smaller fish to be classed as a selective bait for specimen chub. Significantly, most of the big chub caught with maggots were part of a large mixed catch of fish, while those caught with cheese and other baits were either the only fish caught by the angler or were part of a catch composed entirely or predominantly of chub.

THE UNCATCHABLE MONSTERS

Some idea of how difficult it is to catch one of these monster chub can be gained from the experiences of Richard Walker who once found an 8lb 2oz chub floating dead in the river Ouse.

'It was difficult,' he said, 'to know why it had died. Perhaps it was old age; there was certainly nothing starved-looking about it. It had reached an enormous size in a river that has been fished by some of the best anglers in the country.'

Another monster, he reported, could sometimes be seen cruising slowly to and fro through the clear sunlit water but no-one could catch it. 'What it lives on,' he said, 'I really do not know.'

And there perhaps is the kernel of the problem. What do these monster chub eat? Do they feed exclusively on vegetable matter, upon minute organisms like daphnia or upon larvae or nymphs of various kinds? Do they consume molluscs, beetles and other insects? Or do they eat other smaller fish, including their own fry?

Quite probably, they feed—as all fish do—mainly upon the type of food naturally available to them and variations in their feeding habits are related not only to the availability of such food in different rivers but are also influenced by seasonal variations in the abundance of different foods. The indifference with which chub often regard an angler's baits can almost certainly be attributed to an abundance of natural foods or to a process of 'education' as the result of being hooked once or twice during their early years of growth.

So why, it could be asked, do some of these monsters eventually succumb to an angler's bait? Old age and loss of ability to find food probably bring about the downfall of some of them, while others are caught when a shortage of natural foods, brought about by over-population of the water or pollution, causes them to turn temporarily to angler's baits. Yet others are caught when an abundance of offerings from anglers in the form of maggots or other baits results in a temporary loss of their natural caution. Instinctive reaction, similar to that shown by a salmon when it seizes a fly or spinner, may also account for a few succumbing to various baits, but whatever the explanation may be, certainly far more remain uncaught than are ever landed.

BY ACCIDENT OR DESIGN

A study of catches of specimen chub reveals that a high proportion are caught by anglers who were not fishing exclusively for chub, which might suggest that the angler who relies upon luck alone is just as likely to catch a specimen as he who seeks them deliberately. Such a conclusion would however be false, as for every angler who catches a specimen by luck there are many thousands who fish their whole lives through without catching one, and many others who sometimes hook one, only to lose it through using inadequate tackle. In contrast, the angler who deliberately seeks specimens not only finds them more consistently but is also more likely to land them successfully because he is using tackle of appropriate strength.

The odds against any angler catching a real monster are very great but it is possible to reduce them by a considered approach to the task. The first step is obviously to attempt to locate them by sight but if the colour and depth of the water makes this difficult or impossible it is a good plan to fish all likely swims patiently and methodically, using only those baits that are least attractive to small fish. Really big chub can be found in many different types of swim but are seldom far away from a hiding-place. The overgrown snaggy swims that are so often passed by are the kind that big chub favour more than any other.

If chub show signs of wariness to the common baits an unusual one should be tried; either one that can be found in and around the water, such as a small frog or crayfish, or a bait that is completely strange to them such as one of the seed-baits or a meat-bait. This will sometimes bring success when all else has failed.

In those waters where night fishing is allowed the possibility that specimen chub might be caught more easily after dark is worth experiment, especially in rivers that are very clear. There is a definite increase of feeding activity at dusk and the specimen-sized chub are then more likely to be feeding in open water.

Fly-fishing is another method worth trying for specimens. Some real monsters, including one over 8lb, have been caught in recent years, and the fact that some were hooked during the close season does nothing to invalidate the effectiveness of the method.

Richard Walker, who has caught more chub over 6lb than he can remember, has laid down the principles upon which his success is built in his book *Still-Water Angling* and subsequently in articles in the angling press. They are worth repeating and can be summarised thus: first locate the fish; avoid scaring them; use the right tackle; use a bait they are most likely to take; fish at those times when they are most likely to be feeding.

Most of the specimen chub he has caught were taken with the baits and methods described in this book: that is with baits fished upstream or on leger or float tackle. Two weighing 6lb 3oz and 6lb 13oz respectively were taken from the Great Ouse on the same day with a dead frog bait and thirty years elapsed before he caught a bigger one weighing 6lb 14oz and from the same river. The elusive seven-pounder has not taken his bait as yet but, realist and good angler that he is, he does not expect to catch chub of such calibre easily even from such an outstanding chub river as the Great Ouse and is quite content to catch chub of lesser weight on most occasions. Indeed he has often stressed that most would-be specimen hunters set their sights too high and are apt to disparage unfairly chub which, though not specimens by national standards, are truly specimens for the rivers from which they were caught.

11

Experience Teaches

The purpose of this book has been to show that successful angling does not depend only upon methods and baits, luck or that other much misused term 'skill' but upon a combination of understanding of fish and water, observation, timing and watercraft. The experiences related below demonstrate how the practice of these arts can not only add interest and variety to one's angling but also lead to a much more consistent pattern of success. Each experience has its lesson to impart.

The Observed Feeding Pattern

In the course of two successive early morning outings to a favourite river I noticed a big chub feeding on minnows in the shallows adjacent to a thick weed-bed. The feeding time was between 5 and 6am, when the chub would emerge from its hiding-place and move upstream into the shallows. Its ponderous rushes at the minnows were clearly audible and easy to discern in the prevailing low-water conditions.

On the third morning I arrived at the river at around 5am, caught a minnow, lip-hooked it and cast it upstream on a floatless and weightless line. It was taken at once by a chub which when landed and weighed scaled 4lb 2oz.

This sounds almost too simple but success was due entirely to observation of the chub's feeding habits, timing and the right choice of bait. The tackle used was a Mark IV Avon rod, 6lb line and a No 6 hook.

A Change of Bait

I had seen the chub several times on previous visits and had attempted to catch it with a worm and with crust but each time it had refused the bait and shown unmistakable signs of alarm. On this occasion I had a small frog for bait.

The swim was one of those difficult snaggy ones which are often found in small untended rivers and streams. A dense mass of debris blocked the entire width of the stream at the downstream end of the swim while the upstream end was obstructed by an equally dense mass of weed. An ancient willow leaned out over the swim, its branches forming a thin screen and its roots an additional haven for the chub—a formidable combination of obstacles that obviously demanded the strongest tackle.

When I crept up behind the willow the big chub was lying out in open water about two feet upstream of the debris. I could see every detail of it: the thick back, big blunt head and long torpedo-shaped body with its inky fins undulating in the current. It was a splendid fish.

For several minutes I sat watching, awaiting my chance. When the chub fell back slightly I twitched my rod tip and caused the little frog to leap into the water, where it landed with a slight plopping sound close to the chub's head. One sucking gulp from that capacious mouth and the frog vanished. I struck and the rod was pulled over in a long shuddering curve. I held on, knowing that at all costs I had to prevent that chub from diving under the debris.

It almost achieved its aim. The curve of the rod had allowed it to thrust its nose to within an inch of its haven but I had already taken in the slack and now held the fish tethered on less than a yard of line. One quick smooth swoop with my landing-net and the chub was mine. It weighed 4lb 10oz. Miraculously the frog was unharmed—probably because I had struck so quickly the chub had not had time to swallow it.

This success was due almost entirely to the use of a different

H

bait when the chub had obviously become wary of the more common ones. The rest was just stealthy approach and persistence after early failures. Tackle: carp rod, 8lb line and a No 4 hook.

Chub on the Beetle

There had been no rain for weeks. The river flowed low and clear, silkweed festooned the bottom and only the deepest pools contained enough water to conceal a chub. Conditions seemed hopeless but putting my trust in beetles as a bait I chose a fast-flowing but not too deep swim, overhung by an ash tree. Peering through the leaves I could see several chub cruising slowly to and fro just beneath the surface and, unseen behind the tree, I thrust my rod carefully through the branches and lowered a beetle onto the water. At once a chub rose to suck it in and just as promptly plunged into a swathe of weed close in to the bank. Maintaining a strong upward pull I was presently able to draw clear and into the net an exhausted chub weighing 4lb 2oz. I caught no more chub from that swim but did succeed in catching two more with beetles from another swim that was fringed by a reed-bed.

Success on this difficult day was due mainly to choosing swims which past experience had shown to be likely to contain feeding chub and which permitted a close unobserved approach. Tackle: Mark IV Avon rod, 6lb line and a No 6 hook.

Teaching by Prebaiting

When I first tried wheat I knew I would probably have to spend some time 'educating' the chub to accept the new bait. The swim I chose was about 3ft deep at its deepest point and fringed by tall grass—an ideal location from which to observe how the chub reacted.

Several hours elapsed before the first chub started to feed on the wheat. It was soon followed by others until eventually seven chub could be seen feeding. Within less than five minutes

I had caught the first one and although its struggles put the others to flight they returned later and I was able to catch three more with a single grain of wheat.

The success enjoyed in this swim was later repeated in other swims and in other rivers and streams, and clearly demonstrates that persistence and patience are needed when using wheat or other seed baits, since chub cannot be expected readily to feed on such unfamiliar baits until they have had time to sample them. Prebaiting when using those baits is therefore always advisable and essential when using them for the first time.

Tackle: 12ft built-cane rod, 3lb line and a No 12 hook.

Drifting Flake and a Hawthorn Bush

The bank of the small and seemingly insignificant swim was undercut and a small hawthorn bush drooped its lower branches into the water, a trap for debris and drifting weed. Using the drifting flake technique, I drifted the bait down under the bush and it was taken immediately, the bite being signalled by a sudden check in the flow of line. I struck hard and immediately met with the strong resistance that hints at a big chub. It strove desperately to get back into the undercut; then, failing to do so, hurtled into the debris. A few brief seconds of solid resistance when it seemed that I might lose it, then the constant pressure I had maintained prevailed and I was able to pull it clear and net it—5lb 1oz of chub in perfect condition. Tackle: Mark IV Avon, 6lb line, No 1 hook and one AA shot.

The Big Chub from the Stumps

The stumps swim was one that most anglers pass by but it fascinated me and I never missed it. The sawn-off stump of the tree showed only when the water was at normal or low level and immediately behind it was a dark, swirling little eddy of water into which it was possible to lower a link-leger tackle. Unseen beneath the surface were many roots—haunt of many chub and a trap for tackle.

My tackle losses were high but I caught many fine chub from this swim, including several over 4lb. It was one of those places which could often be relied upon to produce a bite when other swims seemed dead and was typical of many similar swims which are always worth trying when the water is low. Mostly I had to be satisfied with one chub from this spot but one evening in March I caught six and lost another when it succeeded in entwining my tackle around the hidden roots. The bait was crust and the chub weighed 3lb, 3lb 2oz, 3lb 8oz, 3lb 12oz and 4lb 8oz, the best catch of chub I ever took from the stumps. (See Plate 3) Tackle: Mark IV, carp rod, 8lb line, No 4 hook and link-leger.

A Lesson in Improvisation

One hot summer afternoon I was sitting in the long grass on the banks of a stream when I heard a splashing sound. Without moving I looked in the direction of the sound and saw two chub lying in a narrow channel of fast broken water across under the far bank. Their dorsal fins and part of their backs were visible above water and their dark tails wavered two and fro in the quick clean flow of current. Both looked to be over 3lb in weight.

Any chance of catching one of them from where I was sitting was slender as between me and the channel there was a solid mass of reeds. It might have been possible to cast a fly over the reeds but the current would immediately have swept it downstream and entangled it in the reeds and even if one of the chub did take the fly there was little chance of hooking and extracting it from the position I was in.

The obvious place from which to present a fly was undoubtedly from the far bank and when I arrived there some five yards above where the chub were lying and screened by tall grasses I tied on a Cinnamon Sedge, stripped about seven yards of line from the reel, eased the rod out over the grasses and dropped both line and fly onto the water.

The fast current immediately carried fly and line away downstream and hidden behind the grasses all I had to do was sit tight, listen for the sound of the chub's jaws and watch for a tightening of the line. The fly was certain to float naturally over the chub and one of them must surely see it.

One did. A splashing sound coincided with the line swinging sharply away downstream and as I tightened quickly there was an instant turmoil of sound from downstream. I stood up to control the chub better and as it sped off downstream at a terrific pace I followed it down, shortening the line by reeling in and maintaining a strong pull to keep it out of the weeds.

That chub hung on for perhaps a minute, boring and struggling, and then surrendered. A fine fish in first-class condition and weighing 3lb 8oz, it was the only one I caught that day and though not a specimen it gave me a great deal of pleasure to outwit and catch it in the way I did.

Chub on a Visible Leger

The chub emerged several times from the thick weed-bed and from just downstream I could see it indistinctly, its dark body distorted and irregular beneath the many boils and whirls in the fast running water. The time was 6am and I had been watching it for some twenty minutes.

Eventually I baited a No 6 hook with a large piece of cheese, weighted the tackle with one swan shot and then cast the cheese upstream so that it landed in the clear channel of water between the weeds, about two yards upstream of the chub. Then I reeled in slowly, holding the rod up so that I could guide the cheese down in between the weeds.

The cheese appeared, bumping downstream over the gravel bottom and clearly visible. The chub moved forward, gave a sideways chop of its jaws and the cheese disappeared. So did the chub. Having grasped its prize it bolted swiftly under the weeds.

I struck hard and held on. The weeds were thick and the

chub had buried itself deep in them, betraying its presence only by shudders that ran up the line, through the rod and into my fingers. Then, abruptly, it gave up and emerged from beneath the reeds shaking its blunt head but clearly beaten. I slipped my net under it and whisked it out on to the bank.

It was the first of a dozen that morning, all taken with cheese fished upstream. Most of them were caught merely by watching the cheese—a useful little trick when the water is low and clear.

TWO BIG CATCHES

Basically there are two ways of making big catches. One is to adopt a wandering style, fishing the bait in all those places that are likely to hold chub; the other is to fish one swim and to use groundbait to encourage the chub to start feeding. I have taken many double-figure catches using one or other of these two different methods.

A March Bonanza

It was one of those fine mild days that are not uncommon in the spring. The sky was filled with high feathery cloud, there was no wind and the river was running slightly above normal height.

My first cast with flake bait on a drifting line into a stretch of fast water brought a chub to the net within the first minute. A few minutes later the line drew taut and I hooked another. I thought it unlikely that I would get any more chub from that swim but tried again and was rewarded with a pull that bent the rod over to its middle joint. In all, I took five chub from that one swim in successive casts, the largest just topping 3lb, and I missed two more bites. Five chub from one swim in the first quarter of an hour was encouraging to say the least.

After that fine start I knew that the pattern for the day had been set. And so it was. From my starting point to the limit of the fishery—a distance of less than quarter of a mile—I took

28 chub within $2\frac{1}{2}$ hours. I estimated the total weight at around 70lb—a remarkable catch for such a small stretch of river. No groundbait was used and all the chub were taken from different swims. It was truly a day when all the time and effort I had put into learning where chub were to be found in different conditions really paid off. Tackle: Mark IV Avon, 5lb line, No 4 hook and flake bait.

The Bridge Swim

One crisp November day I decided to make a serious attempt to catch a quantity of chub from a swim from which I had often caught the odd one while wandering from place to place. It was a deep, quick but smooth-flowing swim, the water eventually swirling powerfully between the metal columns of a railway bridge. I baited it heavily with soaked new bread and then sat down to float-fish it with a slow-sinking flake bait. No bites came until the last hour before dusk. Then the float dipped suddenly and I was playing a chub that I later found to scale 2lb 12oz. It was the first of many, because from that moment on the bites developed rapidly and within the next hour I had caught 23 chub up to 3lb 14oz—a total weight of 58lb.

Eventually I had to stop because although the chub were still biting I could no longer see my float. Nor could I photograph the catch. I have taken other big catches from this swim since but none as large in so short a time. Tackle: 12ft bottom-fishing rod, balsa-wood float and a No 8 hook.

FACTS AND FALLACIES

If one fishes consistently from childhood to maturity, as I have done, one cannot fail to have acquired knowledge born of long experience, to have exposed a few fallacies and discerned a few endurable truths. There are not many of them but they are worth noting.

Success can never be guaranteed; no amount of knowledge about water, fish, techniques, or baits can do that. So aim at achieving some standard of consistency throughout the season and accept some degree of failure as inevitable.

Angling ability is not necessarily related to the amount of time you spend fishing. The angler who fishes *perceptively* can learn more in one season than the angler who spends a lifetime fishing aimlessly.

Do not think you are a better angler than someone else merely because you have caught a bigger chub, or more chub. The best fish you catch will not necessarily be the biggest; nor will it always require greater skill to catch than chub of lesser weight.

Understanding of fish and water is far more important than knowledge of methods and baits and far more difficult to acquire. So devote some of your time to learning all you can about the movements and feeding habits of chub in your chosen waters. Your angling will then improve in proportion to your increasing knowledge of the species.

Do not assume that lack of success means that chub are not feeding. The fault is just as likely to lie in your choice of swim, tackle, bait or in plain bad timing. Learn to mould yourself to the ways of fish, and do not expect that they will always behave as you think they should.

If success does not come quickly—and it usually does not—do not lose heart. Try again and keep on trying until you do succeed, or at least until you are able to establish why you are failing.

The knowledge and understanding you acquire from personal experience will be invaluable but do not scorn the information you can gain from books, which can be of immense value as the distillation of many years of experience by experts in the art.

Fish always on the assumption that no matter how much you learn there will remain much that you do not know and make up your mind right from the start that you want to catch chub and only chub. The catching of just one chub will then mean more to you in terms of progress than the catching of a hundred-weight of other unwanted species. It is better to catch nothing than to catch fish you do not want or had not intended to.

Mention of the part that instinct plays in successful angling is usually greeted with scepticism but after many years of patient perceptive fishing, swim selection, approach, choice of method and bait do all become more or less instinctive. You become sensitive to a river's every mood and in your mind's eye can travel over its every twist, bend and curve in its course, seeing everything as clearly as if you were actually there.

When you have reached that stage and when the other essentials of successful angling have been mastered you can begin to feel that you have 'arrived'. Successful angling for chub—or for any chosen fish, for that matter—could indeed be likened to the bringing together of many different strands of coloured wool, each strand representing a vital factor for success. Only when these different strands have been fused together can you fish in that confident, almost instinctive way that brings consistent success. It can be a long, even a hard road, but it is well worth treading to reach the goal of the complete chub angler.

Acknowledgements

Although this is a book about a favourite fish and as such, relates mainly to my own experiences and ideas, I would also like to acknowledge the generous help given to me by Richard Walker, Peter Wheat, Peter Stone and Geoffrey Bucknall. Thanks are also due to the *Angling Times*, which published so much of my early work, for permission to use news items from that journal and to reproduce the photograph of a specimen chub; to the United States Bureau of Sport, Fisheries and Wildlife and to the German Bundesforschungsanstalt Für Fischerie for information about chub. Also to those many research workers whose investigations have revealed much interesting data about the habits of chub, special mention being made of the work of Dr J. B. Leeming and Dr Chubb of Liverpool University.

Bibliography

Bailey, W. *The Angler's Instructor*, 1857
Berners, J. *Treatyse of Fyshynge with an Angle*, 1496
Houghton, The Rev. *British Freshwater Fishes*, 1879
Leeming, Dr J. B. Paper from the Proceedings of the First British Coarse Fish Conference, 1963
Schartz, F. *The Freshwater Fishes of Maryland*, Maryland Conservationist, 1963
Seaman, K. *Canal Fishing*, 1971
Sheringham, H. T. *An Angler's Hours*, 1902
Walker, R. *Still-Water Angling*, 1953, revised edition 1976
Walton, I. *The Compleat Angler*, 1653

BOOKS OF RELATED INTEREST

Hill, W. M. *Coarse Fishing for New Anglers*, 1975
Rice, F. *Fly-Tying Illustrated for Nymphs and Lures*, 1976
Seaman, K. *Big Fish from Small Waters*, 1973
Wrangles, A. (Ed) *The Complete Guide to Coarse Fishing*, re-issued 1976

Index